"[*A Grotesque in the Garden*] manages to blend the deeply spiritual and personal needs we all have with the ways in which our intellectual reflections can sometimes exacerbate our already fraught condition. It also reminds us that we can learn from one another, and even from fictional characters like Tesque and Naphil, if we would just enter honestly into such deeply personal discussions. While those can be harder to do with real people, the lessons learned from this engaging book can help even philosophers do them better."

— Matthew A. Benton in *Faith and Philosophy*

"This is a delightful book. In terms of genre, it defies easy classification. But like Boethius's *Consolation of Philosophy*, it is at once a gripping story of imaginative fiction, incorporating elements of history, myth, and allegory, as well as a deep and penetrating reflection on the problem of evil and the goodness of God."

— Jeffrey E. Brower in *Journal of Analytic Theology*

"[*A Grotesque in the Garden*] allows for an exploration of philosophical space in a new register and encourages open-mindedness. It also brings an emotional dimension to philosophy of religion that is often lacking in academic writing."

— Helen de Cruz in *Religious Studies*

D1595474

A Grotesque in the Garden

Hud Hudson

Second Edition

WILLIAM B. EERDMANS PUBLISHING COMPANY
GRAND RAPIDS, MICHIGAN

Wm. B. Eerdmans Publishing Co.
4035 Park East Court SE, Grand Rapids, Michigan 49546
www.eerdmans.com

26 25 24 23 22 21 20   1 2 3 4 5 6 7

ISBN 978-0-8028-7817-5

Library of Congress Cataloging-in-Publication Data

Names: Hudson, Hud, author.
Title: A grotesque in the garden / Hud Hudson.
Description: Second edition. | Grand Rapids, Michigan : William B.
  Eerdmans Publishing Company, 2020. | Previously independently
  published. | Includes bibliographical references. | Summary:
  "A short philosophical narrative about an angel wrestling with the
  decision to rebel against God and leave his post in the Garden of
  Eden"— Provided by publisher.
Identifiers: LCCN 2020000624 | ISBN 9780802878175 (paperback)
Subjects: LCSH: Philosophical theology. | Free will and determinism.
  | Theodicy. | Hidden God. | Fall of man.
Classification: LCC BT40 .H835 2020 | DDC 231.7—dc23
LC record available at https://lccn.loc.gov/2020000624

For Xerxes

Contents

Foreword

The book of Genesis tells us that, after driving Adam and Eve out of the Garden of Eden, God stationed "cherubim, and a sword flaming and turning" to guard the path to the tree of life.[1] The wording in contemporary English translations seems to suggest that the flaming sword stood guard all by itself, with nobody wielding it, as in Book XII of John Milton's *Paradise Lost*. But some interpreters put the sword in the hands of an angel, and sometimes the attending cherubim drop out of the picture altogether. One contemporary scholar reports that ancient Christian litanies identified the angel Uriel as the one who "stood at the gate of lost Eden, with the fiery sword." Another explains how ancient and medieval Jewish exegesis led to naming the angel Lahtiel as the guardian of the path.[2]

Literary incarnations of either the solitary sword of fire or an angelic guardian of the tree are, so far as I can tell, rare. Perhaps the most well-known to contemporary readers is the angel Aziraphale from Neil Gaiman and Terry Pratchett's *Good Omens*—a pretty good, but hardly perfect, citizen of heaven who promptly gives away his flaming sword out of compassion for Adam and Eve and then, over the course of the next several thousand years, cultivates a deep friendship with the demon who played the role of Eden's "serpent."

In Hud Hudson's *A Grotesque in the Garden*, the guardian at the

1. Gen. 3:24, New Revised Standard Version.
2. See Anscar Vonier, *The Angels* (New York: The Macmillan Company, 1928), 16, and Saul M. Olyan, *A Thousand Thousands Served Him: Exegesis and the Naming of Angels in Ancient Judaism* (Tübingen: J. C. B. Mohr, 1993), 71–74.

gate is Tesque—a creature of "superior dust" who whiles away his time in the garden reflecting on human beings and their lives as he sees them in visions delivered to him by Eden's tree of knowledge. As we encounter Tesque, he has grown discontent in his isolation and has come to question his divine assignment and his duty to remain faithful to it. In describing his concerns and explaining the fatal decision he is contemplating, Tesque introduces us, his audience, to some of the most philosophically and pastorally important questions one might have about the Christian faith. Other characters, differently constituted, respond to Tesque's arguments. What emerges from their collective thoughts is a portrait of some of the difficulties inherent in trying to fulfill the two greatest commandments—to love God with all one's heart, mind, soul, and strength, and to love one's neighbor as oneself.

This is a splendid book—philosophically rich, beautifully written, and thoroughly engaging. As a teacher of college students, I have found the novel to be an excellent text for introducing undergraduates in thought-provoking ways to key issues in the philosophy of religion. As a lover of good fiction, I have greatly enjoyed spending time with and peering into the minds of the novel's main characters—Tesque, Naphil, and the dog who christens himself "Lazaraistones."

The edition of the novel that you hold in your hands begins with "A Word from the Author to the Reader" that introduces the novel and concludes with supplementary material directing your attention to the variety of philosophical questions and disputes with which Tesque and Naphil are engaged. The supplementary material provides a lot of helpful guidance regarding issues one might wish to raise in a classroom setting or pursue on one's own after finishing the book. This is a terrific resource. But there is much more in the novel that repays thought and attention besides its philosophical insights. Tesque, Naphil, and Lazaraistones are interesting literary characters in their own right, and it is worth asking questions about them, too.

Tesque and Naphil are philosophers; Lazaraistones is not—and happily so. "Hard thoughts," he thinks, are Tesque's business, not his, and he sees that thinking hard thoughts is a big part of what contributes to Tesque's persistent unhappiness. One is put in mind of Socrates's opinion that "the unexamined life is not worth living," and one might well wonder what significance there is in this fundamental difference between Tesque's outlook and that of the faithful Lazaraistones.

One might also wonder why Lazaraistones remains unseen by one of the novel's main characters. The hiddenness of God looms large as a theme in this novel, and so it is hard to resist the thought that we as readers should spend some time reflecting on the hiddenness of Lazaraistones as well. What does this tell us about the character by whom he can't be seen and about the reliability of that character's musings? What significance can we find in Lazaraistones's self-given name and in the way things turn out for him at the end?

There is more that we might ask about these characters—and not just about them individually, but about their relationships to one another and even about how they relate to us, as readers. But perhaps it is best to leave those questions to you now as you join Tesque in his garden and Naphil in her cabin and reflect for yourself on the challenges that emerge from the questions with which they are struggling.

Michael Rea

A Word from the Author to the Reader

A Grotesque in the Garden is a story of two spiritual mistakes, each arising as a different manifestation of the classic deadly sin of sloth—a deep resistance to the demands of love. According to the Christian tradition, we are all the recipients of two great commandments:

> Thou shalt love the Lord thy God with all thy heart,
> and with all thy soul, and with all thy mind,
> and thou shalt love thy neighbor as thyself.

This short novel depicts two individuals who fail to satisfy these commandments in different (yet complementary) ways. Despite the unusual biographies of the protagonists, this is very much an *Everyman* story. With the slightest effort the reader will recognize some similarity between the inordinate self-love and systematic self-deceit which dominates the inner lives of both main characters and features of the reader's own psychological profile. Or, if not, St. Augustine was wrong about the ubiquity of such sin, and the reader belongs to a very select minority, indeed.

The narrative revolves primarily around a particular individual that many of us have been introduced to in another and extremely well-known story, a person exquisitely well-positioned to raise a variety of philosophical puzzles and to articulate a range of critiques both of religion and of religious belief, but without doing so from an atheistic or agnostic point of view. In exploring this person's unique location in creation, the story touches on a number of issues of philosophical and theological concern with emphasis on three main themes.

First, on *divinely permitted evil*: The story presents a new approach to an increasingly popular argument designed to show that considerations rooted in evil should not incline us (to any degree) towards atheism or agnosticism. However, in carefully describing in detail and with precision the relevant defensive weapons that protect the theist in this first and major battle, it becomes all too evident just how they can be turned against the theist in the battles to come. Second, on *divine silence* and *divine hiddenness*: This discussion engages the multifaceted debates centered on the apparent silence and hiddenness of God, and it articulates a novel and worrisome line of reasoning designed to show why it may well be reasonable for creatures to refuse to cooperate with God by way of obedience, even if God exists and is both perfectly good and perfectly loving. Third, on *divine deception*: This portion of the narrative gives voice to an unfamiliar and troubling line of reasoning designed to show how disobedience to God can appear to be the only option available to us which embodies both the right and the good, despite the existence of a perfectly good and perfectly loving God with whose will it clashes rather than conforms.

Just to be clear—I am not advocating all three lines of reasoning, but I have found it liberating to examine these themes with the freedom that comes with the distance of writing from the perspective of characters who differ from oneself. For my own part, I suspect the second and the third lines of reasoning are flawed. Nevertheless, I think the arguments which emerge on those topics are fascinating, and I (for one) don't know where the flaws are located. They are certainly worth taking seriously. The character of Part I does so.

The character of Part II can speak for himself.

The final character of the piece, appearing in Part III, provides commentary upon and criticism of the major themes just recounted, as well as further philosophical reflection on a series of closely linked secondary themes that run throughout the novel—the themes of the effects of sin on desire and thought, self-deception, moral luck, creaturely flourishing, the nature of divine love, and misanthropy.

I began by saying that this is a story of two spiritual mistakes. The character of Part I ultimately fails in the first and greater commandment to love God, the character of Part III in the second to love neighbor. I suspect it is frightfully easy to fail (and miserably so) in both. Each does so, in true philosophical fashion, by being led astray in argument. *A Grotesque in the Garden* provides a sustained example of how certain philosophical arguments can seduce those who are suffering from the effects of sin on desire and thought (and who are thereby especially vulnerable to them) into ruining themselves—that is, on the assumption that they are bad arguments.

PART I

TESQUE

ONE

A Love Letter: From Dust to Dust

I walk in the Garden alone and have so done each day since my internment here began.

I am a coward for not leaving. But perhaps today I shall leave, or if not today then tomorrow. For although I cannot die, I can cease—and a punishment of annihilation imposed by the One who abandoned me here is preferable to the withering charms of solitude in Paradise.

As you will someday be, I too am simply a material thing—a rude chunk of matter—dust of a foreign kind, but nonetheless dust. To dust you will return eventually, for it is not given to you to be immortal in your present state. You will die before you are raised to eternal life. No such respite for me. No peaceful and temporary oblivion but only this uncertain and interminable waiting. I am bound by permanent dust which cannot (save momentarily) be disfigured, torn, or reshaped. I am dust on eternal watch. I am the guard dog of dust.

That common perversion of angels as incorporeal wisps of tenderness and bliss—flitting here and there, mindlessly stroking the hair of sleeping children, moronically dancing on the proverbial pinhead, selflessly rescuing the unwary from invisible dangers, forever converting, counseling, curing, or comforting the whining multitudes, and piously praising the absent One day and night—ranks among the poorest fantasies ever conjured up by your fellow creatures. Know that your father who art in Eden is corporeal, *is* a glorious and imperishable body, but not as distorted by those inexplicably popular and

3

horrific painters of the cherubim, whose artistic vision culminates in portraits of immature little embarrassments looking fat, confused, and heavenward as if their only hope is to have someone happen by and drop a little caramel and faith in their mouths.

I am of the glorious second line in the hierarchy. Mine is a body of terrible loveliness, four-countenanced, unadorned by bruise or blemish or age or decay, a body fierce, strong, and staggeringly beautiful. But unique to my kind, I have not been permitted to employ it in worship or even as chariot or throne of God—that blessed service allegedly reserved for my closest angelic kin. Nor have I been allotted a single hour in the company of my kin. Rather I have been cut away, brought into being only to be separated from my Maker and sentenced to pointless isolation in the Garden. I've even been denied the courtesy of being aware of His presence.

All this time, and I've never even met Him.

◌◌◌◌

I was angry when I wrote that. Daughter, allow me to begin again. I say "daughter" because determining that particular outcome is among the few things remaining under my control. It's not much power, but that's how I'll use it. So, daughter, allow me to begin again.

I stand as a sentry charged with a task of prevention. You and your kind already know me obliquely by way of what you think a myth, a myth developed in your ancient Middle East, addressed to all, and recounted in the Holy Story. The book of Genesis speaks of a privileged and sacred place that played a unique role in the divine plan—of a Garden planted eastward in Eden—and it tells of the fall of two solitary figures from that Paradise. As told to you, the myth represents a series of events in the history of your ancestors. According to that history, these individuals were made just and right and yet in some manner or other freely rebelled and in so turning away from God damaged themselves and their progeny in a way neither they nor any of their descendants could rectify on their own power.

4

Their disobedience was punished by banishment from the Garden and the loss of a certain innocence, immunity, safety, and grace.

Those portions of the tale, I realize, are familiar enough. You will recall, however, that one strand of the narrative abruptly ends upon introducing a character whose fortunes are left unspecified. Yes, I am well aware the Holy Story reports that angels (in the plural), armed with flaming and ever-turning sword, were placed on the east side of the Garden to guard the Tree of Life and to bar any further entrance after its original inhabitants were driven hence—but it's a lie. I alone was banished here.

Or at least I am apprehensive about whether it is true. Perhaps another once stood on the opposite side of the gate, but if so, he chose non-existence over service in the first moments of our assignment and was never replaced. I find that thought disquieting and will return to it in due time.

I believe my imprisonment is undeserved. Or if deserved, the reasons have been well hidden from me. I have stood my ground. I did not fall with the lost angels; I did not turn from God—not yet. Sometimes I have wondered whether my abandonment is deserved for acts I have yet to commit, for transgressions to come. Well, if so (then on the strength of His supreme goodness), I at least have the guarantee I will in fact commit them at some later time; otherwise His justice would be compromised. Some comfort, I suppose.

Still, I remain unsatisfied with this explanation. My freedom, my mysterious and precious freedom, ensures that I am *able* to refrain from future disobedience, even if it should already be true now, in advance, that I *will* not refrain. My freedom is threatened only if I am compelled or forced, only if I somehow *must* rebel, not merely by a true report that as a result of my own beliefs, desires, intentions, and volition I *shall*. Accordingly, suppose it true now that I will later fall, but then, since this pre-imposed penalty for discarding my duty will have been among the causes of my fall, I cannot bring myself to regard my confinement as fitting or proper.

If I do fall from this Garden and carry out my plan, success on my part will surely ensure that you enter the world fatherless and I perish childless. Perhaps I will not be permitted a single step outside the Garden. Perhaps in that instant He shall remove his support from my being, and I shall softly vanish away as would anything so released by the divine hand and no longer attended to by the divine mind. Perhaps my sole attempt at personal rebellion will be thus permanently and quietly prevented. But I simply don't believe a word of it. No—I, too, will be permitted a choice. I will enter the world unobstructed, and I will be allowed the freedom to ignore what I have been informed is my function and to refuse His command. I will be left alone to pursue my own ends, left alone, that is, until my purposes unacceptably cross His. And the cross is inevitable.

Inevitable, for in the event of my leaving the Garden, my whole being will be bent toward one task, the only act of which I am capable that at once may make my own existence finally of some recognizable value to me and also may yield goodness to another beyond measure. Its price is to forfeit my own place in His realm, but, as I have explained, although I obey, I seem to have lost that already. He has forsaken me. Yet I will imitate Him. I will use my will to bring forth new life, though so doing has been strictly forbidden the angels. I will create you, dear daughter, and for this act I will almost certainly pay with myself.

Still, despite missing each other in time, I wish to convey some account of my thoughts and choices and to speak to you here. No one has told my tale. Let this letter be its record.

Even my name was omitted from the Holy Story. I am Tesque. You have undoubtedly been taught to think me under the Hebrew tool *cherub*, a term for the class of creatures especially blessed by propinquity to God. For others of my order in the angelic hierarchy this nearness bespeaks the great joy of intimate knowledge of and precious closeness to God. Whereas for me—it is nothing but a reminder of the unbridgeable proximity to all I want and cannot have, a span so modest but not traversable by such a one as you or I.

I know of my angelic brothers by description, not acquaintance, for as I remarked, I have never once been admitted into their company.

I was not called to duty from my place in the choir. I can boast of no experience of the host of Heaven. My earliest memories one and all have their origin in the Garden as, I suspect, do I. The purpose of this curious provision has always eluded my understanding. Why invest me with knowledge that can only be salt in the wound of my isolation? Why gift me consciousness, rationality, and affect at all? I have been consigned to a trivial task which could be fulfilled by any Grotesque in the Garden, by any soulless and vacant carved stone so positioned that it wards off whatever mysterious enemy is to be kept away. So why gratuitously and cruelly invest what need be no more than a statue with desires and the knowledge of what would fulfill them, only to let its cravings go unattended and unsatisfied? Why cause your faithful statue pain?

My first memories stand out as my most vivid—a turbulent sea of action. I woke to myself, fully formed and equipped with an understanding of my nature and my immediate directive. I stood visible both to myself and to the animals. And all in a moment creation had changed irrevocably, for there was now something that it was like to be the unique entity that is me, to possess my particular center of awareness, to be frightened and bewildered by the understanding that those individuals most similar to me in Paradise had somehow transgressed, and to be subjected to a nearly overwhelming compulsion to drive them from the Garden. My counterpart on the other side of the gate—if the rumor of his existence in the Holy Story is to be trusted—although presumably as new and confused as I, refused to be party to their banishment. But I . . . I unhesitatingly obeyed the command that so powerfully accompanied my creation. Without pause or reflection, I forced those poor creatures from the Garden and closed the gate.

Immediately upon your ancestors exiting this place, the Garden was—how shall I put it?—*raised.* I now lie above you, like an author's pen above the letters on the page (a pen, not an author, for thus far

I have been permitted only the functions of an instrument). And yet for ages now, the Garden and I have been separate from but nearer your world than you might suspect. Your kind cannot so much as point in my direction or reduce the distance between us by a hair's breadth on your own power, but you are lower creatures, and not all directions are open to you. Thinking otherwise is the parochialism of the hands of a clock that imagine there is no direction in which they do not eventually point, since they describe an entire circle when given enough time. You can no more approach or recede from me than the hands of that clock can betray their fixed orbits. North, east, south, west—point those faithful arrows—never out. Left, right, forth, back, up, down—you move in your three-space cell—never towards me.

And again, intolerably, the pointlessness of my quarantine becomes salient. I apparently have little need to prepare to conduct battle to prevent re-entry of the Garden, since it cannot even so much as be found unless your kind acquires the power of movement in my direction or else it is again *lowered* in accordance with the twists and turns of the indecipherable divine plan. But until that eventuality transpires—to address just what threat, exactly, am I so crucially placed on watch?

I have had all I can stand of the five sisters—isolation, alienation, abandonment, loneliness, and solitude. A few words on each.

Isolation is born of distance, and distance is the saddest relation. It carves. It singles. It individuates. Like you, I am placed, I have a location, but I never share it with another. Movement is permitted but contact forbidden. Although I am of foreign dust, I am fragmented—composed of tiny shards and insensible particles, parts cursed with repulsive forces that keep one another and any other objects at bay with all the power and authority of natural law—as, indeed, are you and all creation. In approaching another, my very nature ensures that I merely force it hence—as does yours and all creation's. The thought is simply not sufficiently appreciated; genuine embrace is illusory. Of course, I can achieve an approximation of closeness so as to no longer perceive a distance between my parts and those of my affections, but imperceptible and ineliminable pockets of emptiness still serve to isolate us. Total I wish to mix with another—to enjoy even momentarily the same place, but I am denied even touch. As if mocking my angelic kind, I am always *near* but never fully co-present with another. That exquisite pleasure our Maker reserved for himself and then apparently discarded unused. Omnipresence could afford co-location for each of us, one to another, and yet for reasons I cannot understand this delight has been passed over in favor of mandatory separation. Instead, He has contracted His presence to secure and accommodate my isolation. He has made room for me not by sharing his space but by withdrawing himself, and I—unavoidably, unwillingly, and in his image—can share this world with my fellow living and nonliving creatures only by withdrawing from them in turn.

Alienation is possible in company or in seclusion; it requires only that you are in some manner expelled or prevented from returning somewhere or reuniting with someone or someones to whom you belong. I enjoy none of the pleasures of being amongst my angelic brothers; *they* are my people, not these stones and this dirt. Still, just as this Garden gate effectively bars entrance to the world, so too am I so securely and remotely locked away that I am not even marginalized, for I am not even on the page. The pain of alienation intensifies when, rather than resulting from some accident of fortune, it is caused by a misuse of will, by being intentionally wronged as when, in His infinite wisdom, God marooned me on this island-Garden for reasons that He has not seen fit to share with me.

But I see I have become angry again. I should take back the remark about the misuse of free will. I should say rather that in my *abandonment* I have been harmed rather than wronged, for God (unlike the rest of us) cannot fail to perform His moral obligations. Of course, not all intentional harmings are moral wrongs, but the harms hurt all the same, especially when they are prolonged and inexplicable and originate in someone you believe loves you. Was there no other permissible alternative available to Him that did not require my abandonment here? How could my sorry corner of the world possibly be a non-negotiable moment of the divine plan?

Loneliness is a felt experience, a complex emotional state, an unsatisfied desire for togetherness. It is unpredictable, unpleasant, independent, and of its own mind. Perhaps it will join in force with isolation, perhaps it won't. You may find it keeping company with alienation or wholly absent from that condition, supplanted by indignation or rage. It can worsen abandonment or be altogether indifferent in the face of betrayal. When it does arrive, however, it dominates. One's entire landscape, internal and external, is painted in its muted and unhappy colors. Even goodness loses its magnetism, and what is beautiful seems distorted. But I realize I hardly need to explain loneliness to you or to anyone. It is our one shared inheritance. No one honest can consider it a stranger.

Solitude is the only member of the quintet not inherently disvaluable. Where the other elements burn and injure, solitude could be a balm and a restorative if only it were occasionally punctuated with interaction. Solitude harbors hidden treasures—the reintegration of a fragmented self, a gradual discovery of one's deepest values, an enriched harmony with one's environment, the autonomy made possible only through freedom from all engagement with and responsibility to others. Yet this deep and awesome well can run dry. And I—well—I am replenished enough. Already I know myself and what matters to me all too clearly. I am perfectly attuned to this my paradisiacal prison. The harmony cannot be improved upon, but the music is dying.

In passing the endless cycle of seasons, I walk the Garden. Your sun no longer shines upon this ground, but the Garden glows with its own light, and the brightening and dimming of the light is my day and night. The river flows under the walls into the Garden and then out again, who knows from or to where or how? The flowers and trees bud, bloom, beautify, fade, drop petals and leaves, and naked, shiver in the silent shadows of the dark snows of a Garden Winter only to find new colors in the crisp air, fresh breeze, and warm rain of a Garden Spring.

Morning after morning I begin by tracing the same intricate path. Along the way I touch the same flowers on the same petals in the same order and every hundredth step is twice the distance of each of its ninety-nine predecessors. It's not as if anything harmful can befall me or visit corruption on the Garden should I forget a flower or misstep the path, but one needs the ritual of patterns, and I have systems from which I must not stray.

I spend afternoons wading and confessing to the patient but uninterested river, letting its waters wash over me as I recall with longing the exquisite beauty and vitality of the once-present but long-departed animals. I pay my respects by reciting with fond remembrance the names of the twelve I christened when we so briefly shared the Garden together. Those were the twelve who on at least one occasion saw me, and it is so very good to have been seen by anyone or anything. I cared for them. There are nearly four hundred and eighty million different ways to recite their names in order, twelve thousand of which I achieve each day after stepping into but before exiting the river. The sequence requires almost a century and a decade to complete, yet I have brought the circuit to its end more times than I care to remember.

Evenings are occupied in appreciative fascination, perplexity, and most often sorrow—in a fashion I will be able to describe momentarily.

Profoundly black, unspeakably still, and sleepless nights crawl by while I compulsively calculate and classify everything: I count days. I count hours. I count seconds. I count colors. I count sounds. I count odors. I count tastes. I count textures. I count memories. I count desires. I count fears. I count hopes. I count questions. I count uncertainties. I count types I count. I count pains.

I count my friends, whose number is two. My first and oldest friend is mathematics. Individual numbers and shapes, of course, are not friends, but I have found they are companions. The sublimity of their relations to one another is as inexhaustible as it is inexpressible, penetrating (to my modest capacity) the depths of those relations fills me with awe, and the momentary release I experience from losing myself in those discoveries the closest thing I know to joy. Her equations call to me, her certainty cheers me, unveiling her structure delights me, her subject matter exhausts and bests me, and her necessity and immutability reassures me there is always some goodness in the world of which I may partake no matter where I am.

My second friend is the magnificent and awful Tree. Not of Life. Her I leave alone. I speak of the Tree of Knowledge, my only living companion in the Garden who is also aware of me. He is my nourishment and my window out of Eden. I eat the succulent offerings of his branches and thereby come to see in all its splendor and sordidness the details of your world. Of your multicolored history I am a transfixed and devoted student. Thus do I spend each evening by his side watching the passings of your wretched and wonderful lives. I am an expert on cruelty; I've seen its many faces, and I can't look away. But also how often I have witnessed inexplicable sacrifice and mutual caregiving. How such events ever surface amidst such misery is a mystery, and yet there they are time and time again. What a tapestry! What a world weaved of time and chance, horrors and beauty, suffering and love!

I know the Tree is aware of this and wills our one-way communication, but he does not join. I speak, and he remains silent. I sing, and he remains silent. I plead, and he remains silent. I pray, but I remain silent. Still, I count him my second and only other friend.

Shall I describe for you a recurring fear? Just as my brothers the seraphim have been closely linked with love, we cherubim have been intimately associated with knowledge. And yet, sometimes, in the midst of my longing for companionship, I suffer doubts and uncertainty and fantasize about whether God has created only myself and the Garden and whether there is anything at all where the river water rushes as it disappears under the Garden's walls. Foolish, of course, but the thought persistently and irrationally continues to reassert itself. Could it be that this infernal Garden exhausts all of creation? If so, otherwise unanswerable questions about why He would permit your world to remain so deplorable in so many ways and why He would not interfere with the sickening ruin of so many of His beloved creatures might receive a simple answer: God *doesn't* permit those atrocities; they aren't real, for the extent of the cosmos is the extent of the Garden, and I am genuinely alone and deceived.

Don't misunderstand me: I don't doubt and never have doubted His existence any more than I can doubt my own. In fact, I don't think such doubt is possible for one of my nature. But certainty stops there. Where is He? Why create an entire world and then play the truant? What would be the point? Why bother to call thinking matter into being, instill in it an insatiable desire to unite with its source, and then hide like an ill-mannered child while it suffers unto death?

But then what would such a hypothesis make of my own situation? Are the visions afforded by the Tree simply magnificent illusions, brilliant but fabricated scenarios of a fictional world all designed to test or to torture me? No, I can't seriously entertain that my private torture could be His object, but His aims (whatever they are) are impenetrable. And, as for the alternative, to what possible end would I be tested? To see how long I will blindly obey without explanation or direction? How much value could be embedded in discovering the answer to that? Enough. These reflections are embarrassing. Obviously, your world is real and others with whom I might interact—my glorious and angelic siblings, your pitiful and wonderful race, the simple and loving brutes—do exist. I am not some sort of unique and meaningless experiment, and my longings have real rather than imaginary objects. I hereby refuse to indulge or nourish such thoughts of quasi-solipsism any longer.

It's just that I've been denied companionship for so very long that I've even wished to exchange duties with the Messenger of Death, thus ensuring at least some communion with all creatures, however brief. His is such a sublime charge—to share in each person's last moments while providing comfort and tenderness.

Enviable—Angel of Death, not for the kill, but for the kiss.
One's holy task—on each bestow the loving touch of lip on lip.

But for all that—he is where he is, and I am where I am. And once I fall from this place, you will come into being and be where you are.

TWO

Lazarai Stones

Before I take leave of these flowers and grasses and waters, I would like to offer you a record of my motivation—what I have learned from millennia of private thought on my peculiar situation and what I have learned from watching the bleak yet hopeful inhabitants of your world through my communion with the Tree. Perhaps I can help you appreciate my reasoning in a way that will justify my choices to you.

My time here has been characterized by nothing if not by obedience. And what have I gained? Naught that I can tell. Leaving is as easy as inserting the key into the gate and walking beyond the Garden, a simple and intentional course of action, completed in a moment, with consequences for eternity.

Let me distinguish myself from those who rebel only after confusing themselves about whether He exists. Of course, when the confusion is successful, they do not call it rebellion (for how can you further separate yourself from, or stand in any relation at all, to something that does not exist?). But rebellion it remains whether called by its own name or by another. The most widely successful attempts at such confusion arise from reflections on evil, which (to my mind) have almost no force whatsoever in their most common dress and presentation. As you will see momentarily, grounds for rebellion can be so much more surprising and sophisticated and tempting.

I would like to present three thoughts to you, each by way of a story: The first thought—*on divinely permitted evil*—to explain to you why considerations rooted in evil should not incline us at all towards atheism or agnosticism. Of course, showing that they should have no effect on *you* is really the more important demonstration, since as I mentioned earlier, I believe my angelic nature itself prevents such inclination. Like the demons, I, too, believe and tremble. But your nature is not so constrained, it is consistent with disbelief, and I wish to close this avenue to that mistake for you. The second thought—*on divine hiddenness*—to explain to you why it may well be reasonable for me to refuse to cooperate with God by way of obedience, even if God exists and is (as the Holy Story incessantly reminds us) perfectly good and perfectly loving. The third thought—*on divine deception*—to explain to you why turning from my assigned duty in disobedience may actually be the only option available to me which embodies both the right and the good, despite the existence of a perfectly good and perfectly loving God with whose will it clashes rather than conforms.

On Evil

As I realize I revealed earlier, my forced isolation has made me angry towards God. I can't hide it; I am angry with Him. But I have reserves. I can endure this anger and alienation and limp along through my days of seclusion. I am made of superior dust. Frightfully many of your kind, however, appear to have so much more reason than I for righteous anger. Look at your world. Should you feel betrayed?

God loves you, yes, but as I write this letter, a tropical cyclone with winds exceeding a hundred and fifty miles per hour strikes the region you call southeastern Bangladesh. Over a hundred thousand of your brothers and sisters are killed, another ten million rendered homeless, and untold numbers of frightened, injured, and innocent animals suffer and die along with their human fellows.

And yet the destruction and ruin of that cyclone is only a drop in the ocean of suffering that characterizes the history of your world. For numbingly long stretches of time, generations and generations of confused and terrified creatures have torn one another limb from limb in a daily struggle to minimize the pain of hunger, earning nature her description of being red in tooth and claw. Rational animals, deluded by disordered desires, have compounded the suffering (in profoundly significant ways) by bringing intelligence and cruelty to the table, dominating one another, and inventing astonishing and revolting ways to reveal new depths of suffering. And nature itself, not to be outdone, has contributed a steady stream of avalanches, blizzards, droughts, earthquakes, floods, hurricanes, tsunamis, volcanic eruptions, and wildfires. Moreover, given a bit more time, an asteroid or comet strike will be sure, in a whirlwind of destruction, to take from you all you've managed to achieve these last few centuries.

Uncontroversially, my daughter, there is abundant evil in your world. Occasionally, you will find a few pathetic attempts to pretend otherwise, but they are always either infantile or else disingenuous. Of course, it goes without saying that some evils are justifiably permitted (when, for example, every option open to you contains some evil or other) and that other evils can contribute to the production of great goods distinct from themselves (when, for example, the pain of treatment leads to the pleasures of health), but neither of these mundane observations serves to show that evil is somehow really absent from the world; indeed, the truth of either observation guarantees its presence in some measure. Alternatively, one may feign skepticism about the existence of evil on the grounds that one lacks a compelling and comprehensive theory of value, but you need no grandiose theory to correctly and justifiably recognize the specific disvalue arising from the cyclone. Arguments for atheism grounded in evil can be defeated, but not by a hopeless, head-in-the-sand ruse of pretending there is no such thing as evil to begin with.

Alas, once evil is unmasked and you learn to see it everywhere—for it is everywhere—the atheistic worry is not far behind and not hard to characterize. It was raised, if inchoately, by your first parents. It is as old as your race. If God exists, He is omnipotent, omniscient, and perfectly good, and thus the magnitude, intensity, duration, and distribution of the horrific and inscrutable evil that mars your world appears to generate an immediate case against Him. Why? For if He existed, by His omniscience, He would know (or foreknow) where evil exists (or is about to exist without His intervention), by His perfect goodness, He would be sufficiently motivated to eradicate (or prevent) that evil, and by His omnipotence, He would be able to do what He knows how and is sufficiently motivated to do. That is, such pointless and gratuitous evil would not exist for long (or would not exist at all).

The briefest glance at your history, however, reveals an exceedingly long, violent, and chilling tale of what certainly appears to be a story with pointless and gratuitous evil at its very core. Accordingly, concludes the evil-monger, God does not exist, after all.

And that—in short—is the primary case against Him, the case that has taught generations of your kind that there is nothing of excellence above them either to obey or to disobey and that a turning toward governing themselves and dependence upon their own ingenuity and power is not a simultaneous turning away from their Creator.

The initial reply to this worry should be obvious enough. Obvious even to a child. Doesn't the success of the complaint depend on whether there are good reasons—morally justifying reasons—for God to permit the magnitude, intensity, duration, and distribution of this horrific evil, inscrutable though it appears to us? And, let me confess, although I am manifestly and vastly superior to any of your kind in the powers of intellect, much of the evil is wholly inscrutable to me, as well. Even I cannot fathom its function. Yet perhaps such evil is permitted by God because it has a compensating good. That is, perhaps permitting this evil (or something else equally bad or worse) is a necessary condition of securing some good, and (other things being equal) the combination of the good and evil together is better than their mutual absence. Or perhaps the evil is permitted by God because He has some other morally justifying reason for neither eradicating nor preventing. It doesn't all have to be accounted for in terms of goodness; there are, to be sure, other sources of moral permissibility than sheer value.

Yes, the initial response is an obvious (even tedious) one, but then those under the spell of this argument quickly tend to lose their way and those to whom the argument is addressed tend to lose their footing. That is, at this first interesting juncture, the standard exchange (conducted, as it so often is, between novices) often falls to pieces. Why? Realizing that the existence of such a morally justifying reason would undermine this brand of atheistic reasoning altogether, its would-be proponents issue a pointed challenge to the faithful—"So, just what is the putative morally justifying reason for, say, the cyclone?" (which, as I sadly learn from the Tree, continues to wreak havoc as I write). The proponents lose their way, because they have lost sight of the rules of the dialectical situation they have created. Remember (as they sometimes do not) that they have presumptuously proclaimed to be in a position to convert believers into nonbelievers, that their chosen strategy has assumed the form of an argument rather than non-intellectual enticements, and that the success of that strategy depends upon the premises of their argument, one of which now transparently stands badly in need of support—namely, that there is no such morally justifying reason for the relevant evils. Defending that premise is the responsibility of the proponent of the argument. The foregoing challenge which attempts to shift that responsibility to the believer is a strategic mistake. Allow me to explain.

Suppose those targets, the believers, are not in a position to identify the relevant morally justifying reason in question. Suppose they are wholly at sea in the face of such an inquiry, that they do not even know where to begin in reply. (And, let me add, despite the number and variety of their clever and heartfelt and woefully unsatisfactory attempts at theodicy—bless them—this more or less seems to be their position.) What would follow from that? Not that this atheistic argument is thereby a success! Who could imagine that an *inability* in one's opponent to demonstrate as mistaken some premise upon which one crucially depends is somehow a good and justifying reason to think that premise is true? As if justification for one's substantive beliefs could be secured merely by exposing the inadequate capacities of the untutored to refute them! Let the believers among you happily admit ignorance here.

Let them swear they have no clue what the morally justifying reason for the world's evils might be. Why care? The real question is whether the champions of this line of atheism can move from your honest concession that you do not know of a morally justifying reason to the further and considerably more telling claim that no such thing exists. They cannot.

Recall that I promised you a story. Here's one to help show that they will not be able to transform your ignorance of a morally justifying reason into a positive and persuasive case for nonbelief. A real story. From your own forgotten history. I have it of the Tree:

Long, long before your birth—although it doesn't matter when and it doesn't matter where—a ragged and bone-tired people established a village bordering on a lake in what is now the Western Siberian Lowland. Subsistence farmers, without means of irrigation, their lives depended on the pattern of the rains. Patterns vary, and the rains did not come. Crops failed, and the rains did not come. Children died, and the rains did not come. A superstitious people, they made sacrifices they could ill afford, and the rains did not come. In desperation, the eldest member of the village, sagacious and correctly regarded by all as exceptionally virtuous, entered the lake and offered herself in exchange for the rain, which came immediately and in abundance.

According to the lore that followed, the lord of the rain, Lazarai, just then flying with his great wings above the village, saw and accepted the life of the elder in exchange for the life-sustaining water, and out of respect for her sacrifice wept three tears which fell amongst the rain. These precious items were the Lazarai Stones— teardrop shaped, ice smooth, one inch in height, and forever oscillating through the color wheel in hue. Or, rather, that is how they would appear to any person who was both sufficiently pure at heart and sufficiently wise. To anyone else, they would have the appearance of nondescript, indifferent pebbles of the sort that litter the shores of the lake in the hundreds of thousands.

A Lazarai Stone was said by the villagers to have great power, for it could guarantee the return of the rains from year to year, and it could slow the aging process of anyone who possessed it from a setting of the sun to its next rising. Happiness awaited whoever found one. Children playfully hunted the stones in the Spring at the planting festival, a few adults made serious searches throughout every season of the year, and no one in the village was so confident that the stones were merely the stuff of legend, that he or she refrained from scanning the ground carefully and discretely whenever unfamiliar ground was underfoot.

Time passed and friends and families quarreled over whether the stones were genuine. Believers were challenged by nonbelievers to produce them, a task the believers could not perform. In turn, the believers replied that their ignorance of the location of the stones did not amount to a reason to think that they did not exist, not unless it were a truth that if there were Lazarai Stones, the villagers would be aware of them and recognize them as Lazarai Stones.

Now once the disagreement had progressed far enough to arrive at that particular insight, the villagers had stumbled upon something enormously significant, although its significance escaped them. But it need not escape us. Daughter, suppose it were true that if there were Lazarai Stones, the villagers would have been aware of them and recognized them as Lazarai Stones. Then, since they manifestly were not aware of anything they recognized as a Lazarai Stone, the nonbelievers could have simply combined those two basic facts and declared victory in their dispute. The point upon which both parties should have focused, but did not, was whether they had any good reason to believe this key supposition *was* true. They had the ability to do so but not the happy accidents of thought that would have led them to the realization I intend to present to you now.

To begin, it is important that you not think that this story is about whether Lazarai Stones really are lying on the shores of a lake, undiscovered, somewhere in the Western Siberian Lowland. To get that matter out of the way, they are not. There are no such objects, and there is no lord of the rain, winged or otherwise.

The point isn't about the stones, it's about a style of reasoning that can be found both in the story of the Lazarai Stones and in the argument from evil I am warning you against.

The argument against the reality of the Lazarai Stones requires a seductive but false step. No one, not even the superstitious villagers, should agree that, if there were Lazarai Stones, they would be aware of them and recognize them as Lazarai Stones. It is an easy matter to see why the claim appears tempting, at least initially, for although the villagers did not exhaustively survey the entirety of the area where the rain fell (and so where the tears would also have fallen), they carefully and thoughtfully searched so very much of it that they may have become increasingly confident that if the stones were anywhere, they would have been uncovered and recognized by now.

But that tempting defense fails twice over. Why—you wonder? For two independent reasons.

First, the villagers (quite understandably) searched where it was possible for them to search—on the land. They searched the fields, the village, the roads, the plains, the low hills, the lakeshore, and were rewarded with only the ordinary fragments of rock to be discovered anywhere by anyone. They did not (equally understandably) search where it was not possible for them to search—on the bottom of the lake. The lake is deep and wide and inhospitable, and rocks, even magical ones, sink. In the local region where fell the rain, however, much more of the surface was water than land. Accordingly, it is more likely that if tears had dropped from the eyes of Lazarai, they would be at the bottom of the lake rather than exposed among the rocks of the land. This is not to say that there are Lazarai Stones. I remind you, no such things exist. Instead, it is simply a correction of the incautious endorsement of the key supposition: Despite the long and careful search of so much of the land, there is not good reason to think that if there were Lazarai Stones, the villagers would be aware of them, for it is quite likely that if there were such things, they would be precisely where the villagers were unable to search.

Second, and of equal importance, suppose that Lazarai Stones were real and that improbably they had happily fallen on the widest part of the path from the village to the lake in a configuration that would be easily seen by any villager making the daily trek for drinking water. It would then undoubtedly be true that if there were Lazarai Stones, the villagers would be aware of them, but there is not yet reason to endorse the key supposition, for we do not have the further guarantee that they would be recognized as Lazarai Stones. Surely you have seen a bird, and not recognized it as a bird until it took flight. One can perceive without correctly classifying; it is commonplace. The legend of the Lazarai Stones insisted on a special feature of those artifacts. To the impure or insufficiently wise, they would appear as ordinary rocks, not distinguished in any way. Only the genuinely pure and wise would discern their true shape, texture, and ever-changing hue. Perhaps the self-sacrificing elder could have marveled at such splendors, but no one in the village had reason to think he or she passed the requisite tests. Indeed, each was wholly in the dark about whether anyone at all in the village could recognize the stones for what they were. Accordingly, even if the Lazarai Stones were real and had, in fact, been objects of mere awareness, the villagers had no reason to presuppose that they would have recognized or correctly classified them, for given their ignorance of their own states and abilities, they had no reason to suppose they were capable of such an achievement.

That is the story of the Lazarai Stones and that is its lesson. The nonbelievers in this case were right, but their reasons were inadequate; neither they nor the believers should have taken those reasons to have any force whatsoever. But you and your kind, daughter, are in the same situation. In the case of God, the believers are right and the disbelievers wrong, but that is not my present point. I remind you—I am not here mounting any sort of argument for God, and, of course, many of your kind will continue to disbelieve on other grounds that do not center on evil. I wish only to help you see that the most popular reason for disbelief fails in a similar way and, again, to close at least this avenue to that mistake for you.

The atheistic argument from evil worrying so many of your kind similarly requires a seductive but false step. No one, not even your philosophers, should agree that, if there were a morally justifying reason for the cyclone (which continues to rage unabated as I write these words), they would be aware of it and recognize it as a morally justifying reason. As before, the claim appears tempting, at least initially, for although the intellectuals in your history did not survey the entirety of possible reasons (of which, unlike the bounded area where fell the rain, there are infinitely many candidates), they carefully and thoughtfully searched so very many of them that they may have become increasingly confident that if such reasons existed, they would have been uncovered and recognized by now.

But this tempting defense fails twice over, and due to the same considerations we have just seen with the Lazarai Stones.

First, your intellectuals (quite understandably) searched for morally justifying reasons where it was possible for them to search—amongst the states of affairs whose contours they could imagine, properly articulate, reliably represent to themselves, and critically inquire into. They did not (equally understandably) search where it was not possible for them to search—amongst the states of affairs that were too complex for them to imagine, articulate, represent, critique, or even so much as form a dim awareness of. The realm of possible reasons is deep and wide and inhospitable to minds as essentially limited as yours (or even my own), and morally justifying reasons may be as inaccessible and deeply submerged in the waters of complexity as you please. The range of reasons that your kind might, shall we say, *sample*, are, to put it mildly, exceedingly modest. Or, to be fair, they are impressive enough given your particular roster of capacities, but exceedingly modest nonetheless. Thus, despite your long and painstaking search into the labyrinth of value for compensating goods or other morally justifying reasons, there is no good reason to think that if there were such things, any of you would be aware of them, for it is quite likely that if there were such things, they would be precisely where your intellectuals are unable to search.

Second, suppose that there is in fact a morally justifying reason for the cyclone and that it consists in some familiar state of affairs involving the existence of rational beings in your world, a state of affairs that has been reflected upon to some degree by nearly anyone marching through life's journey. It would then undoubtedly be true that if there were a morally justifying reason, you and others would be aware of it, but that is no more a success than before. Consider the species of morally justifying reason I earlier termed a compensating good. Just as the Lazarai legend laid down special conditions on those marvelous tears of stone, so too, a compensating good requires properties that are not as transparent or as easily recognizable as one might wish. To the insufficiently insightful, it would appear an ordinary state of affairs, not much of a justifying reason for anything of interest. Only the genuinely magnificent of mind would discover the requisite necessary connection to the permission of those evils that follow in the cyclone's wake and also discern its exceptional degree of value which renders it compensatory, that is, which makes the combination of the good and evil together better than their mutual absence. No one among you has reason to think your mind magnificent enough to penetrate the modal and axiological mysteries here identified. Indeed, each of you is wholly in the dark about whether anyone of your number could recognize a compensating good for what it is—even Accordingly, even if the morally justifying reasons were real and had, in fact, been objects of mere awareness laid at your feet as it were your kind—*and my kind*—simply have no reason to presuppose that we would have recognized or correctly classified them, for given our ignorance of the range of our own mental capacities, we have no reason to think ourselves capable of such an achievement.

Harping on evil is not a royal road to rebellion that passes through the safe haven of atheism.

THREE

The God of Silence

Of course, it is not as if anyone should pretend that the existence of God is somehow demonstrated because the problem from evil is discovered upon examination to be toothless; many a failed argument has a true conclusion. But, as I said before, in this case the believers happen to be right, and neither believers nor disbelievers should take appeals to evil of this variety to have any force whatsoever in support of the opposing verdict.

Significantly, however, in my reflections I have come upon rather different reasons for disobedience—*considered rebellion, reasoned rebellion, respectable rebellion, warranted rebellion, worthy rebellion*—reasons that need not be erected upon the confused and impossible soil of atheism. Let us not ignore Him. Let us address ourselves to His absence and to His character. Other stories from your world will assist us in our endeavors.

On Hiddenness

One kind of evil (if it is evil at all) exists only if He does—divine silence. You and I, daughter, are supposedly designed to love and to enjoy Him forever. Doing so, I am sure you have been told in reverent tones, is our greatest possible good and our single most significant purpose. Yet how strange that so many of us never seem to be participating in this good. Instead, generation after generation is conceived in which nearly indistinguishable individuals live nearly

interchangeable lives replete with times to plant and reap, kill and
heal, break and build, weep and laugh, mourn and dance, cast away
and gather, embrace and retreat, acquire and lose, keep and discard,
rend and sew, be silent and speak, love and hate, war and make peace
. . . and yet from cradle to grave there is no special time set aside for
blessed delight in His explicit and unambiguous presence, the sole
experience which allegedly could furnish the only sort of genuine
satisfaction and contentment of which we are capable by design.

And what magnificent substitute rises to take its place? In lieu of
what, exactly, is this unsurpassable good of union with Him absent
from nearly every one of His creatures that inhabit your world, absent
even from the slavishly devout who seek Him tirelessly in earnest,
in fasting, in prayer, in penitence, in cell or wilderness, in desert or
cave, in (of all things) *solitude*, and plead for this their function to
be fulfilled at the expense of every other good the world offers?

Witness a handful of representative substitutes, drawn from the
archives of my memories of horrors revealed by the Tree:

A sleep-deprived hunter slips on the icy ledge of a cliff. The fall
shatters his leg, bones protruding from the skin. His bow lies out of
reach and even he can smell the blood with which he is announcing
his presence to the animals of the night. He does not keep his promise and reappear at the door of the hut where his three children and
their mother are huddled together over the last of their firewood,
starving. He does not even last long enough to be bitten and torn,
for as the temperature rapidly drops he freezes to death frightened
and fearing for their safety as do they nine days later while fearing
for his. And where is God?

The hull is breached, and the water begins to rise in the cabin
where the mother has just nursed her infant and rocked her toddler
into an uneasy sleep on the highest berth. In minutes the water will
touch their bodies and startle them into panic with its coldness. For
a few minutes more they will scream, gasp for breath, flail for her, and
tiny lungs will fill with the water that reaches to the ceiling. Standing
now to her waist in the numbing sea she frantically prays, yet the first

set of minutes passes so much more quickly than the second. And where is God?

Her twins have escaped the attention of those who report on the maturation of the slaves until earlier this week when they were discovered, prodded, and groped by two men sent from the central house. She tries to intercept the men as before, to entice them, to seduce them, anything to prevent their gaze from falling on her girls, but incessant labor has diminished her youth and her features have lost whatever power they once possessed to distract men from their duties. Now she stares vacantly as her terrified children, barely fourteen, are marched roughly up the path, stumbling in long, flower-print dresses, the first new dresses they have ever seen. And where is God?

A young bride watches, thunderstruck, as soldiers pull her husband from the train and into the mud, taking first his hands, then his ears, then his eyes, then his head. The men laugh, drink, spit, and toss his left hand at her window so forcefully that the wedding band cracks the glass. And where is God?

Their grandmother is not a witch. She does not cast spells; she merely suffers from a stammer with which she has been afflicted since first she could speak. She cannot understand or reply to their questions and accusations. She thinks they have come to help her. She repeatedly tries to kiss the hands that hold her forcefully still so that the powerful demon the minister believes inhabits her will not have the opportunity to strike anyone in the crowd. She believes they are now supporting and lifting her, helping her to a location where she can appreciate whatever wonderful thing the people have come out this evening to see and to share. She mumbles a few words of gratitude. She mistakenly believes one of them is her son. The fire is lit beneath the stake to which she has been tied. And where is God?

The whole town is here. A few men and women still strike semi-defiant poses, but hunger will consume their defiance within the week. Others huddle together, backs turned to the guards, wild with fear, trying not to attract the thin eyes of the one who has already fatally struck two of them with a spade this morning without provocation and without warning. They are informed that they are all to be executed in one month's time, in sequence, in the presence of the invading queen. Each wonders who among them will be chosen last, the sole witness to the genocide of his people. And where is God?

And so it continues, seemingly without interruption or end. In place of all creatures loving, worshiping, and glorifying God together and in fellowship under the comfort and protection of His holy presence and majesty—the whole supposed purpose of breathing life into this vice-ridden horde of dust and then bestowing upon it an irresistible longing—His creatures instead raise their arms against one another in a circus of cruelty as far removed from love as one can be and together lift their voices with angels and with archangels to proclaim, "My God, my God, why have You forsaken me?"

All this tragedy so magnified by God's absence . . . and yet atheism is not thereby revived. To the extent that we focus just upon the various harms that befall us creatures when we knock upon the Lord's door only to be answered by silence, we simply encounter the problem of evil in a unique form. And so we dutifully rehearse its proper solution.

But then why is He absent? Why does He not attend to the world's horrors and to the victims of such unspeakable suffering? Could it be that He doesn't have the power to reveal himself? Absurd. Could it be that He doesn't have the wisdom to understand how much value would be generated by His presence and the comfort it would afford those in pain and despair? Absurd. Could it be that He is not good enough to care about our welfare and our happiness? No, but the focus on goodness strikes somewhat closer to the truth, as I will attempt to explain below.

But then again, daughter, just what ought we to have expected of perfect love and perfect goodness to begin with?

Attempts to predict the manifestation of perfect love and perfect goodness by appeal to the imperfect and fallen parent/child relation is a pitiful error. I suspect your kind imagines itself at its finest in the sort of love felt and bestowed upon your children, and maybe you are correct in this, but your best effort in this arena is a paltry and immature thing, hardly a blueprint for divine love. That you manage to occasionally suspend some of your selfish tendencies and to periodically love your children in the way you should love every neighbor is partially to your credit (partially to His) but still so shot through with self-love and self-favoring conditions that to pretend you can read what course of action He will or should choose off your own checkered and inconstant performances as parents is laughable.

Even worse is the appeal to friendship. He is not your friend. Nor is He your enemy. Friendship requires a minimal proportionality, not merely love, and that is a feature neither you nor any of the angels can ever aspire unto. Some humility, please . . . your mind and intellectual capacities are closer to the complete absence of consciousness, closer to a rough slab of granite than they are to the divine mind—as is every finite mind no matter how powerful and wise; any natural number is better likened to zero than to infinity—any natural, for on that never-ending staircase every finite number is small. Of course, the persons are friends: the Father with the Son, the Father with the Spirit, the Son with the Spirit, but it ends there in an eternal and permanently closed friendship of Three. No fourth may ever enter and none of the Three may ever depart. Even if your clumsy and broken notion of friendship could provide insight into how the Three may relate amongst themselves, it does not give you license for prediction of how His perfect love will be manifested toward you or toward any other part of creation.

But again, then, what ought we to anticipate from perfect love and perfect goodness? May we claim some entitlement to sophisticated and multifaceted interpersonal interaction? May we insist upon being provided with His comfort in times of extreme grief and sorrow? Or, if not upon comfort, upon His silent presence or at least the presence of His shadow? Or, if not upon His presence, at least upon sufficient evidence for belief in His existence equally available to one and all of His suffering creatures? Or, if not upon sufficient evidence, at least that He will act in ways that will be aimed at the best interests of us—His dearly beloved?

I have come to believe that no such anticipatory demand is justified. Allow me to explain myself.

First (and more easily addressed): The expectations of multifaceted interpersonal interaction, of comfort, of presence, and even of sufficient evidence for belief are all subject to the same maddening but perfectly adequate reply.

God has several purposes, most of which are known only to (and can be known only by) the divine mind. To be sure, His perfect goodness and perfect love ensure that our welfare is numbered among those purposes. Owing to His perfect goodness, God never does anything morally wrong, He has an unsurpassable set of moral virtues, He always acts on proper reasons and with appropriate motivation, and He is inclined (but not necessitated) to create and sustain good states of affairs and to prevent and eradicate bad states of affairs. We have significant moral standing as angelic and human *persons*, and thus we have a place in God's decision-making; how divine action affects us matters from a moral point of view and from the point of view of the production of value, and thus our interests must be taken into account in His preference structure and as He exercises His terrible and omnipotent will.

Despite our standing, however, not all our desires are certain to be fulfilled nor is it guaranteed that we may enter into His presence, if our doing so were to conflict with another and more important goal that He may permissibly pursue. Moreover, pursuing this goal need not be at our expense; indeed, it may be ultimately for our benefit. (More on this theme and its alternative momentarily.) Nevertheless, I believe myself (and your kind) to be as inescapably ignorant here as we show ourselves to be when fruitlessly searching out morally justifying reasons for the cyclone. Still, let me report to you suggestions from your own kind as to what those purposes might be.

Why does God not engage us in a wide range of interpersonal interaction of the familiar sorts we value and enjoy with one another? Because His doing so, even for the briefest span, would so overwhelm and devastate us in such an unadulterated form that we would no longer be capable of interacting with one another. A flash of even moderately intense light can blind the eye and permanently impair the capacity of sight; how much more would unmediated interaction with God, interaction that the innocent foolishly cry and clamor for, impede every function they possess? God has no interest in reducing us all to idiocy.

Why does God not comfort us adequately even with His mere presence or, barring that, with whatever diminished presence we can tolerate—as I suggested before, with His shadow? Perhaps He desires us to suffer in ways that are inscrutable but ultimately in our best interests to experience and overcome. Perhaps He foresees a great good in our seeking Him in certain ways or in our helping one another to seek Him and thus strengthening and improving ourselves and our neighbors. Or perhaps He foresees a great evil in those who would even more forcefully reject Him in their present state and lose their greatest good forever. Finally, if I were forced to take sides with these guesses of your theologians and philosophers, I would hold with those who say He wants your rebellious kind to fully appreciate how awful things are when (with His absence) He reluctantly grants your fallen request to exist on your own terms without obedience to Him, all for the purpose of properly preparing you to cooperate in reconciliation through His mysterious plan of atonement, a plan the details of which I cannot understand even with the assistance of the Tree.

Once again, though, all such speculations are voluntary. There is no pressure to claim any insight on the matter. Perhaps He simply has other goals which are beyond our ken, and there is no reason whatsoever to presuppose that if there were such goals at cross purposes with His continued presence in our lives, we would be aware of them and recognize them as such. As I said before, thus far we have something so similar to the general problem of evil, it may be combatted with the same weapons.

So, too, for the further question about why God (allegedly) does not provide adequate evidence for belief in His existence. Here I simply cannot join with you. I have no empathy on this issue. The evidence to my mind could not be clearer, and temptation to disbelief or suspension of judgment is one obstacle my angelic nature prevents from ever coming in my path. I imagine the evidence is available to you as well, if it was not somehow stripped from you in the fall, and if the evidence is evident, then it is certainly your sinful nature that prevents you from appreciating or admitting to yourselves its potency and force. But I shall postpone the promising consideration that your unbelievers are at fault for their own dismal state of disbelief due to the workings of sin in their cognitive lives, since so many of your kind take such offense at the idea that they cannot entertain the suggestion adequately. Instead I remind you first that freedom is a tremendous good and that unless beliefs are possessed on the right grounds (grounds perhaps prevented by the sort of imaginary evidence in demand), those beliefs may be fixed by fear and all subsequent behavior coerced in such a way that the tremendous good of freedom will be forfeited. And I remind you second that even ensuring belief with a certain evidential pedigree may be at irreconcilable odds with His goals for the atonement in some fashion the explanation of which is wholly unavailable to you and me.

Second (and to my mind, far more troubling): Consider even the *least ambitious* expectation—that in the cosmic silence of divine hiddenness He will certainly watch over us in love and act in ways that aim at our best interests. This seems at once both to impose only the slightest demand and also to be the most reasonable, but this expectation, too, may be overreaching and grotesquely in error.

Again . . . and slowly . . . *even the minimal expectation that He will act in our best interests may be grotesquely in error.*

As illustration of my warning, I present you with another story of your past from the Tree:

The ship has been trapped in the heavy ice for a few weeks now. Provisions are running low and only a single seal was caught and butchered before the rookery disappeared from sight. The captain is sailing home with the most valuable cargo his ship has ever carried, a woman—daughter to the king and wife to the general—thought to have been kidnapped and put to death in an invitation to war. It is a mistake; instead she attempted escape with a lover and has been caught. Reaching the familiar harbor of his home city before the army begins its march inland and the navy sails north will correct the misconception and save thousands of innocent lives.

The ice is thick and the occasional warning of a cracking timber like a cannon blast reminds the crew that the ship is powerless to resist the expanding force of solid water. Attempting to shorten the trip by straying into the pack ice has already taken a personal toll. After burning the furniture and storage boxes on board, the captain offered up to the fire eighteen heavy wooden carvings that had been passed through his family line, keeping the crew and the ship's dogs from frostbite and holding death at bay for the last three days. Essential pieces of the ship will burn next if it does not first splinter and sink below the surface of the ice.

The captain loves the ship's dogs. They share a name with his ship, and he has always been closer to and more at ease with these faithful creatures than with any human companion. He has seen this moment coming with a dread unmatched by anything he has experienced in fifty years of life. Circumstances constrain choices. The crew is starving and his decision is both clear and the source of the most severe pain and anguish he ever feels.

Three-quarters of the crew have now disembarked, hiking the floes to find seal, when the ice imprisoning the ship suddenly breaks. Before noon a channel forms to the open water and it is now or never. Leaving will strand the men searching for food, men the captain admires, trusts, and loves. They will die a terrible and painful death on the ice, abandoned and alone in their attempt to serve the ship and follow the orders of its captain. Staying will forfeit the opportunity to prevent the needless war in whose path there will be many and far more terrible and painful deaths than on the ice. Sailing into the open sea the captain allows his thoughts to dwell on those he loves and leaves behind, regretting that he cannot secure both goods before him which, given his options, are in conflict.

This rough and seasoned captain, although he would be unable to say so with any degree of sophistication, is a man of love. He loved his homeland. He loved his crew. He loved his dogs. He even loved his ship and the carvings that tied him to his childhood and to the childhood of his father. Unlike most of his fellows, however, his loves were well ordered.

Individuals—whether things or events or experiences—have value or disvalue. And value comes in degrees. To love perfectly is for one's love to be in the right proportion to the object of one's love, everything considered. The carvings were precious but did not have the value of the lives of the crew and dogs, and in letting the fire consume the carvings for the sake of the crew, the captain did not fail to have the right relation to those adored art objects. The dogs did not have the value of the crew, and in taking their lives and their flesh for the sake of the crew and not for the dogs' own good, the captain did not fail to properly love the dogs as he should. The lives of the hunting party did not equal in value the lives of vastly more individuals unavoidably in the path of the war about to commence, and in abandoning those men on the ice for the sake of preventing the war and not for the good of the hunting party, the captain did not display the defect of imperfect love.

Perfect goodness guarantees concern for the beloved and generates strong desires for the beloved's good. Perfect love, however, need not be determined by such concern or desire and need not always aim at what is best for the beloved. It all depends on how circumstances constrain choices. Omnipotence not to be found among his features, the captain's choices are constrained by contingencies as base and simple as ice flow and human miscalculation in interpreting the unexplained absence of a woman. God, of course, is not restricted by any such contingencies and bows only to necessary connections, connections as immune to the omnipotent will as is the truth that four is equal to the sum of two and two or that the genuinely free have the ability to disobey.

Imperfect love is found only in loving too little or loving too much. Don't misunderstand. Perhaps love is the greatest relation and perhaps the love commandments—to Him and to neighbor—can bear the weight of both a comprehensive theory of value and a comprehensive theory of obligation. I am not saying that it is a mistake to put love first in all things. I am suggesting only that some goods can be secured only at the costs of other goods, and imperfect love is demonstrated by those whose affections for the lesser goods dominate in such a way that the proper order is perverted by the accidental preferences of love. If the captain had been too attached to the carvings or to the dogs or to his shipmates, he would have loved too much, but the defect exhibited would not have been in putting love first or giving the demands of love priority; it would have been the defect of love privileging the wrong objects.

Why does your kind so confidently assume that you could not be in the position of the ship's dogs? *Deeply loved* . . . favored and cared for with a love that surpasses your understanding, a love so magnificent that should your greatest good be unrealized and your function and purpose left unsatisfied, it would yield in Him the most severe pain and anguish He ever feels. And yet, not due to contingencies that omnipotence could sweep aside with a decree, but owing to necessary conditions that put two goods in competition for realization, He uses your lives and takes your flesh and frustrates your flourishing for the sake of the higher good and not for your own sake. Doing so does not impugn His perfect love. And whether the constraints of necessity require Him to do so is a fact about which you are as utterly in the dark as you are about morally justifying reasons for the cyclone, or for His hiddenness, or for centuries of divine silence.

I wish to bring this second of my three thoughts to a close. The problem of evil confronts us with lives that have been ruined and destroyed, lives whose subjects may reasonably judge were better not to have been lived at all—if that is all there is to them. But suppose we grant that there is a morally justifying reason to permit such ruin. Divine hiddenness shows that the morally justifying reason does not require God to be present to those who have been thus ruined; they may well suffer in divine silence. Reflection on perfect goodness and perfect love further suggests that the morally justifying reason may not even require God to provide individual compensation in the life of the world to come, nor even a place at the table in the world to come. The wages of cooperation and faithful service may be annihilation. Many of God's creatures may be instruments only—dearly beloved, yes, but not to excess—loved with a love befitting the well-made, sentient wheels and cogs in the divine plan.

Daughter, it is one thing for it to be permissible for Him to use us as mere instruments, tools to be chipped and broken in the service of a foreign good and then discarded without adequate and individual recompense. But it is quite another for it to be obligatory for us freely to consent to such treatment in submissive obedience. Perhaps His overall goal is unsurpassably good—as I imagine it is—but morality does not require that *you or I* act so as to maximize the good. Morality permits a certain concern for ourselves as well. I am allowed to trade maximization of an impersonal, cosmic good which would come at the cost of my own ruin for a minimal degree of self-realization and some small measure of happiness. To be loved (perfectly but only to a threshold), then spent, depleted, ruined, and destroyed—why on earth (or in Paradise) freely cooperate with that?

"But you are speculating," you exclaim. "Even if what you describe were an option He could permissibly pursue, the fact remains that He won't behave in these ways."

But, daughter, if doing so truly is consistent with His perfect goodness and perfect love, why not?

"Because He has made promises to us. He has revealed His plan. He has told us so."

FOUR

Divine Deception

I agree in part—He has made promises to us. He has told us so. But has He revealed His plan?

On Deception

Thus far in my manifesto for deserting my post and leaving the Garden unguarded, I have merely exposed the feebleness of one source of alleged justification (in the case for atheism from evil), and I have explained why I may be permitted to not cooperate with God, why I may not *wrong* Him in quitting his service even though he wishes such cooperation from me.

Permission alone, however, does not generate desire or sufficient motivation, and even if I would forfeit no moral obligations in leaving both this Garden and my tiresome solitude behind, I may not have yet convinced you of the attractiveness of doing so, all things considered—of exactly why I intend to select that course of action. Yet one staggering consideration remains for me to give voice. It has haunted me as I have served my sentence in Paradise. I cannot see my way around it.

Once I realized that the case from evil was so infirm precisely because it presupposed capacities and powers that I—like the villagers in search of Lazarai Stones, like you and your kind, like any mind short of God's—was completely in the dark about whether I possessed, I also gradually came to understand that we each suffer a common vulnerability that has curiously been neglected. I know that I am not in a position to justifiably determine whether, if ever finally confronted with them, I could recognize His reasons for permitting the horrific evils of the world or comprehend the explanations for the revolting consequences of His protracted absence, His hellish hiddenness. I have come to face and to accept the unhappy situation that such reasons and explanations may well be beyond the ken even of the angels. But I have discovered that my admission of this fact has unsettling and underexplored repercussions.

I am getting ahead of myself again. Let me start with a story, one of the first glimpses of your world ever revealed to me by the Tree:

As instructed, a young boy of thirteen appears in his yellow burial robes in the doorway of the luxuriant inner courtyard of the principal counselor to the emperor. Wide-eyed, he looks at his surroundings illuminated by moonlight with a mixture of amazed wonder (in having never seen the counselor's private and hidden chamber until now) and abject fear (from overheard servants' whispers about the three-day siege on the city walls protecting the palace from the barbarians of the East). The blind counselor hears his approach and welcomes him with warmth.

Finding his courage, the boy inquires why he has been summoned at the midnight to these rooms and why he has been clothed in his burial robes. Through the labored breathing of the aged counselor he learns that he must travel unexpectedly this night and that the thick and heavy burial robes were the only dress available on such short notice to shield him from the fierce elements of the Winter solstice.

The boy is frightened. The yellow robes mean death. They have always meant death. And he knows that for three days now death has been vehemently striving on the other side of the city fortress, screaming in a foreign tongue, furiously searching for any opening to enter the palace and take everyone there. He speaks his mind, revealing his fears to the counselor.

In turn, and with great compassion, the counselor explains that his fears are indeed reasonable. The uninvited guests do wish his torture and his death, but they won't have it. He reminds the boy that the emperor is powerful and has selected him for a special purpose. He is to reunite with the emperor in safety and to love and enjoy him for the rest of his days, which will be long. Of all the children in the palace, he is the special one who bears the image of the emperor, he is the favored and chosen one, and the emperor will not let him come to harm. The plan of escape is without flaw, but he must do exactly as he is told, and he must do it now.

Escape will require nothing more of him than to consent to a specially prepared meal of bread and wine, the consumption of which will place him in a deep and untroubled sleep from which he may be reawakened and reunited with the emperor after being safely and swiftly carried through the night and away from the palace by the royal guard. The counselor takes the boy's hand and leads him to a table set for two, offers him his choice of place, and explains that he will share this last meal with him as a goodbye, for they will not be permitted to travel together on this journey.

This news is nearly too much for the boy to bear. The counselor has been the boy's constant companion from his earliest memory. He has provided for him, watched over him, played with him, challenged him, laughed with him, encouraged him, taught him, and loved him. Separation seems unthinkable. Yet the boy has never known the counselor to make a mistake in judgment. His wisdom, everyone acknowledges, is unrivaled and his character unsurpassed. He would never knowingly fail the boy in any way.

The boy pauses. The bread and wine have a peculiar taste. Merciful poison? Is this a quick death to prevent a terrible loss of dignity and certain torture? No, he firmly reminds himself, its nature has already been revealed by the counselor. The odd taste signals nothing sinister; it is but the lingering sting of a medicine that will induce the sleep which mimics death, a temporary and peaceful rest from which he will awake in the presence of the emperor. They eat together in the quiet stillness of the night, the counselor with his hand gently resting on the boy's knee.

Over the half-hour span of silence in which they slowly share their last meal, the boy is troubled by a series of private and disturbing thoughts. He does not for a moment doubt the counselor's knowledge; the old man surely knows whether consuming the meal will cause him any harm. He does not for a moment doubt the counselor's devotion and goodness and virtue; neither would the old man fail in his moral duty to the boy in any way. And he does, indeed, sincerely believe the old man's pronouncement; he anticipates he will soon sleep a deep sleep. Temporarily at ease, he looks to the reawakening and to his life with the emperor to come.

And yet, as the boy fights to keep his eyes open, he gradually comprehends that even if these judgments of his caregiver's knowledge and goodness are correct (and they surely were) it is not enough to *ensure* that he has not been deceived (as I learned from the Tree he, in fact, had been, for the wine was poisoned, the walls were breached, the enemy was searching the palace, and the emperor had been dead twelve hours).

That is enough of the story. I now wish to show why I have come to believe that you and your kind and I and my kind may all be cast in the role of the boy, and I wish to draw out the consequences of this, our mutual predicament. Doing so will take some time and some effort of you.

I predict for you a Christian affiliation, given both the part of the world in which you will march through your childhood and the strong inclination to theism which my blood will nearly certainly contribute to your cast of mind, and that religious tradition (along with its closest relatives) has maintained that among the sources of knowledge available to human beings you should recognize divine revelation. Details differ amongst Judaic, Islamic, and Christian variants on the Holy Story but in ways that don't matter much for my purpose. But let us take up the example of your own Christianity in the following reflections, a religion in which (with a few dissenters here and there) the historical and contemporary view declares that God has revealed certain truths touching on matters of consequence to all human persons near and far, past and future, and that these truths are not ones you and your kind could have fully discovered left to your own devices.

Several models for divine revelation of truths (as opposed to the revelation of God himself) have been put forth: Sometimes the proposed mechanism is causal, effected perhaps by dreams, or visions, or some sort of direct manipulation of the chemistry of your animal brain. Sometimes the truth is manifested in some person, some bit of behavior, some miracle, or some other magnificent chain of events. Sometimes the revelation is portrayed as a kind of divine testimony—addressed and spoken to an individual or to a people and communicated directly in His own voice, or by prophet, or by inspired scripture. In whatever fashion it eventually gets transferred to you, such testimony takes the shape of an assertion of fact, and the force of the reminder *alone* in the phrase "knowledge by revelation alone" is simply once again to signal that your human powers of cognition—reason, understanding, imagination, sensation, introspection, memory—are not up to the task of discovering the truth or falsity of these assertions on their own. Apart from His revelation (if there is such a thing) you do not have any independent means of verification or any significant epistemic access to the relevant subject matter.

Although your theologians always contest particular examples, candidates for such items of knowledge by revelation alone include claims regarding the fall of humanity, the trinity, the incarnation, the atonement, and the general resurrection and life of the world to come.

"We look for the resurrection of the dead and the life of the world to come." Thus ends your Nicene Creed with a reference to one of the most central teachings of the Christian faith. Similarly, your Apostles' and Athanasian Creeds explicitly and prominently call attention to the resurrection of the body. Let us term this doctrine *the general resurrection thesis*—the revealed and splendid news that every human person who has ever died will rise again from the dead—and let this announcement stand as our example of a candidate for knowledge by revelation alone.

Now, a simple moral lesson: You will, I trust, acknowledge that being deceived is a bad state of affairs and that lying is morally wrong. But that's too coarse. A more careful pronouncement is that there are some features of being deceived that are of disvalue (say, a mismatch between one's cognitive states and the world) and that lying is *prima facie* morally wrong (that is, that there is some genuine moral reason not to deceive others). Nearly everyone, however, recognizes both that deception can be extrinsically valuable (for it can lead to substantial goods such as saving the deceived from making a life-ruining mistake in a moment of passion) and that the moral presumption against lying can be overridden by even stronger moral reasons in favor of deception on a particular occasion. As anyone can quickly see, however, these *prima facie* obligations can easily come into conflict with one another, and when they do, the directive against lying quite obviously is not always the most stringent, overriding consideration in moral decision-making. In short—lying is not always wrong; it depends on what other morally significant factors are also at stake in the circumstances.

Your problem (*and mine, for the angels must join you in this*) is straightforward. Consider that general resurrection thesis, that promise of a new dawn on which so many of your kind have pinned their hopes and around which they have arranged their lives—or consider any other piece of alleged knowledge by revelation alone that better suits you—and let us give it a name, *K*. Moreover—and here is the startling concession upon which so much turns—simply grant without protest that the testimony inviting us to adopt K as a truth has come directly from Him whom we know to be both omniscient and perfectly good.

Behold now the shadow which darkened the boy's mind in his last moments with the blind counselor and with which you also are now confronted:

Do we thereby have knowledge of K? Not if K is false—if K is false, then we too stand in our yellow burial robes, full of hope, yet success-fully deceived by someone who knows that K is false.

Do we have a way of verifying the truth of K and exposing a deception, if deception it be? Not if K is a genuine candidate for knowledge by revelation alone, for earlier we specified we do not have any inde-pendent means of verification or any significant epistemic access to the status of such candidates.

Do we have a guarantee that God would not deceive us about whether K is true? Not if our being deceived about K is the kind of bad state of affairs for which there exists a compensating good or morally jus-tifying reason. And doesn't it all seem so clearly, so obviously, to be of a piece with our inquiry into the cyclone? If there is a compensating good or morally justifying reason for such deception, God's perfect goodness is in no way impugned by the deception—on the contrary, it may be morally obligatory for Him to so deceive us.

Do we know that there is no such compensating good or morally justi-fying reason for us to be deceived with respect to K? Not if we are among those who found persuasive the defensive maneuver for undercutting arguments from evil to atheism that I explained to you earlier on the model of the Lazarai Stones. Consistency would require a claim of ignorance here just as before and for more or less the same reasons.

Unhappily, then, our claim to knowledge of K seems to be threatened: Neither your kind nor mine can without reservation trust such divine pronouncements—even if we simply help ourselves to the certainty of the background truths that God exists, that He is omniscient and perfectly good, that He has graciously provided us with His testi-mony, and that we have interpreted that testimony aright. And once we have lost this particular kind of trust in the testimony, it cannot be the source of testimonial knowledge.

Given the centrality and importance of the claims which figure as candidates for knowledge by revelation alone, this line of reasoning points to a severe and underappreciated problem confronting us all. O yes—"He has made promises to us. He has told us so." But are we properly dressed in yellow robes all the same?

Perhaps you think the worry comes to nothing, that it can be easily avoided on the commonly held grounds that God simply cannot tell a lie, since doing so either invariably betrays a kind of weakness or else is always morally wrong and since His perfection is incompatible with both defects and moral wrongdoing. Moreover, the Holy Story contains scores of passages in which lying and deceiving are subjected to heavy criticism and condemnation, and many of your historical theological champions—your Augustine, your Gregory the Great, your Aquinas—were apparently all united in an absolute prohibition on lying.

Still, I believe you will discover that this alleged flood of support is all too frequently hedged and that it contains hidden qualifications that make the prohibition rather less severe than it seems at first blush; for instance, the prohibition does not usually extend to all cases of deception but peculiarly only to the special case of deception known as lying. As I have just reminded you, however, knowledge by revelation allegedly comes on the world's stage in a variety of different costumes, only some of which involve the sort of direct assertion that is subject to the charge of lying as opposed to some other form of deception.

Moreover, many of your theologians have noted (and sometimes lamented) that the Holy Story is also a source of evidence both for the claim that God Himself has perpetrated (whether directly or indirectly) an intriguing assortment of lies and deceptions as well as for the claim that such behavior was laudable and morally permissible.

Furthermore, historical support of a universal moral ban on lying furnished by influential institutions and religious traditions is frequently qualified by the presence of excepting clauses. For example, the hard rule against lying has been occasionally softened by an accompanying definition of the term *lying* which insists upon "having the right to know the truth" as a necessary condition of being successfully lied to. The prohibition, then, would be silent in cases in which the right had never been present to begin with or else had been either waived or forfeited. In a similar fashion, by imposing surprising and implausible restrictions on what counts as a lie, your theorists were able to consistently advocate an absolute ban on lying (thus peculiarly construed) while acknowledging the permissibility of some instances of deliberate deception by way of explicit assertion known by the speaker to be false. And *that*, once clarified and exposed and impoverished, amounts to no support at all. Compare the fact that an influence as powerful as the Church itself could also stand in favor of the prohibition against murder and yet endorse the permissibility of deliberate killings in certain cases of self-defense—not because such actions are permissible murders, but because they do not fall under the scope of the proper analysis of the term *murder* at all.

Daughter, are we not in fast agreement that it would be an impossible morality that maintains that deliberate killing in self-defense when innocent lives are at stake is acceptable moral behavior but that lying to achieve the same ends in those very cases would be inexcusable, unqualified, moral wrongdoing?

Finally, it is dialectically inappropriate to mount a defense of an exceptionless duty to refrain from lying by appealing to the very sources whose veracity has been called into question. If you are (in fact) being lied to by your friend (and for your own good), and you come to suspect that this might be the case, I doubt you'll make much useful headway in an attempt to discover your predicament by asking your friend if he is lying to you. Similarly, if the context in which the question arises of the permissibility of engaging in direct and intentional deception by way of false assertion is one in which the Holy Story and the authority of certain figures is presupposed as reliable and trustworthy ground, then you only face the problem of arriving at the correct interpretation of those sources. But that is decidedly not the context in which the question is being raised here.

This hopeful initial response to our predicament—that God never lies—would have to be founded on independent moral reasoning rather than any circular appeal to knowledge by revelation alone (whose reliability, after all, is currently under suspicion). And after turning to and inspecting that independent moral reasoning, it should be irresistibly clear to you and to anyone that despite the disvalue of being misled and despite the *prima facie* wrongness of lying, the moral presumption against lying can be overridden by even stronger moral reasons in favor of deception on a particular occasion. Once again, then, moral reasons for action can come into conflict with one another, and when they do the directive against lying quite obviously is not always the most stringent, overriding consideration in moral decision-making.

Let us abandon that line of reply; it fails. Perhaps, instead, you believe that my worry can be avoided on the grounds that whereas God can tell the occasional lie, He simply cannot deceive us about something as important as the fall of humanity, the trinity, the incarnation, the atonement, or the general resurrection.

In other words, perhaps you entertain the response that prohibition need not concern the telling of lies as such, but rather the telling of certain lies rather than others. But why? What, exactly, is the difference? Is the idea that the consequences of being deceived on such momentous topics would be so severe, so unfathomable, so utterly bad, that despite the intellectual humility ordinarily manifested by those of us who wonder in admitted ignorance about what might justify God in his permission of the world's other evils, we can quite clearly discern that an atrocity of this magnitude just could not be justified?

This answer cannot stand. We do not command such selective powers of insight just by wishing it so. Such a reply is misguided twice over:

First, it is a half-hearted (and vulnerable) position which professes ignorance about how much we know about just which things are good, about just how good they are, and about the necessary conditions of their realization (when thinking about the problem of evil in general), but changes its tune in a few special cases to declare that something like divine deception about the general resurrection just couldn't be tolerated. Whence this confidence? I suspect it might have its origins in the plausible intuition that we know (for example) that there could be no morally justifying reason to permit a world consisting of nothing but creatures in devastating pain at every moment of their existence.

But even if we do know God could not admit such a pain-only world (and I grant we do), note that this extreme scenario is not at all relevantly similar to the case of divine deception with regard to the general resurrection that we have been investigating. Appreciate, if you have not already, the wealth of information hidden in the "nothing but" qualification in the phrase "nothing but sentient beings in devastating pain at every moment of their existence." In particular, that phrase has the effect of simply stipulating a scenario in which no other factors (apart from those entailed by that description) are relevant to determining its overall value or justifiability. Perhaps, under the guidance of that ideal stipulation, we would be in a privileged position to see that such a world is inconsistent with God's nature, but there is no similar guarantee of the absence of other relevant factors in a case of divine deception about the general resurrection, and absent the absence, we have no business temporarily departing from our ignorance concerning morally justifying reasons to make confident pronouncements about the intolerability of divine deception on the matters of revelation.

Second, the proposal screams with overexcited hyperbole. Would such deception be bad? Well, yes, of course. Would it be *this* bad—the *worst*—disvalue in the highest? No. You and all human persons are material beings—dust. What if it were true that despite the many ingenious proposals articulated by your philosophers for reconciling materialism for human persons with the doctrine of the general resurrection, they are one and all terribly mistaken and this union is simply impossible? What if it were true that a material thing cannot be raised from the dead? God would, of course, know this . . . and yet perhaps even temporary and fragile creatures of dust, creatures essentially barred from enjoying any sort of afterlife, creatures not in fact made to love and to enjoy Him forever, creatures like *you* are worth creating anyway, and moreover, *ought to be deceived on exactly those points.*

To be clear, whether you have in fact been deceived in this way is not the point at issue. To get that matter out of the way, I am not denying that you are (as I am) a material object, and I am not denying that materialism for human persons (and for angelic bodies) is consistent with the general resurrection, and I do not contest that you may look for the life of the world to come. Yet I do not presently endorse or have much faith in that promise either. My present concern is only to emphasize that if (like the child at his bread and wine) you are wrong and God has successfully deceived you about the prospects for things of your kind, I just can't see that the deception component of your situation is as bad as the world of unrelenting and devastating pain or anything else so wicked that we somehow know it could not be permitted by a morally justifying reason.

But let us abandon this line of reply as well, and return to our thoughts of the boy and his counselor. The old man had always been a divine friend to him. Of course, that adjective has to be taken in context. The aged counselor was not God, but he wasn't wholly unlike God, either. The counselor and God share some properties relevant to recognizing him as the fine caregiver he was, and perhaps they share other properties, as well, properties that would have enabled the counselor to impart knowledge to his charge by way of sincere testimony despite the fact that the boy realized that he could not unqualifiedly trust everything he had to say. It is crucial to understand, however, that the boy's lack of complete trust need not be based on any failing of the counselor's; indeed (as I just intimated) it may be predicated on the respect in which the old man resembled God— namely, on his substantial portion of knowledge and goodness.

Permit me to take a liberty with the story. As I have it of the Tree, the deception was successful and the murder was intended as a kindness to prevent a worse fate. Suppose, though, the emperor had survived, the guards knew of a route for safe passage in the night, the bread and wine concealed only heavy drug rather than death, and the testimony of the counselor had been in all respects honest and true. Still, the circumstances from the boy's point of view would not have been altered. He would still have been faced with the very same considerations whether his eyes were closing in death or merely in sleep.

Recall that the boy is confident that the counselor knows which scenario is real, and the boy rests assured that the counselor has his best interests in mind. The boy knows that the counselor has other goals, too; in particular to prevent their capture and torture by the enemy at the city walls. He is aware that the counselor understands that deceiving the boy would have disvalue and that lying to the boy would be *prima facie* morally wrong, and yet even a child can recognize that the counselor nevertheless may also have had other *prima facie* duties, other moral reasons in favor of misleading him that were even more stringent in those circumstances.

But now we shall envision our story with a different conclusion: Whereas in the historical story revealed by the Tree, the counselor lies and joins the boy in a meal of death, in the version I ask you to consider in its place, the counselor foretells a genuine plan of escape and tells the truth in every particular.

Now I ask you, daughter, a subtle question: In the story thus reconfigured, is the boy's claim to knowledge of his impending and successful rescue imperiled by the fact that he could well understand how the counselor (while knowing the facts of the matter) might have been lying to him as a manifestation of his own goodness?

Just to be clear—of course he didn't achieve knowledge in the historical case, for as the Tree teaches, he was successfully deceived and his beliefs were false. The question I am putting to you—and consider it carefully—is if history had conformed to the story I put in its place, would the boy then have had knowledge by way of receiving the counselor's (true and known) testimony, despite his realization that there may well have been morally justifying reasons for his being a victim of deception on that occasion?

Perhaps you think the answer is obviously affirmative and furthermore that if the boy can gain testimonial knowledge from the counselor in the face of such uncertainty and doubt, surely you and

I could receive similar knowledge from God's revelations. But how persuasive, on reflection, is transferring that reaction in our new story to the case involving God's promises to either of us, human or angel? The problem I wish to expose to you now lies in a feature in which the counselor is utterly unlike and wholly inferior to God but which surprisingly makes it all that much easier for the boy to acquire knowledge by way of the counselor's testimony.

Revelation is testimony, and testimonial knowledge is a problematic and delicate thing. Your and my trust in God's promises hangs by a precarious thread, indeed. How should we conceive of such promises, of divine revelation, of testimony in general? Is it somehow a basic source of justified belief (on a par with perception and introspection and memory) requiring little to no effort from the recipient? Could it really be an innocent-until-given-grounds-for-guilt affair such that in the absence of relevant objections, anyone may justifiably accept a piece of testimony merely upon hearing it? No, surely that is too simple. Knowledge of the world is a precious and fine achievement and not so cheaply and easily acquired. To my mind, the more plausible view of testimony requires something in addition to the mere lack of undercutting considerations in order to impart justified belief in its subject matter. But what else, exactly, is required? Must the additional ingredient be some (non-testimonial) good reason for thinking that testimony is generally reliable or trustworthy or merely a (non-testimonial) good reason for thinking that a particular instance of testimony is reliable or trustworthy?

It doesn't matter—adopt the weaker, local requirement, if you wish: The boy had a plausible chance of meeting that additional standard in his interactions with the counselor. After all, they were cast of the same human mold, possessed of the same cognitive powers, and so relevantly similar on a wide variety of measures. The boy was extremely well positioned to get good evidence from perception, memory, induction, reason, and the like relevant to a judgment of the reliability of the counselor on the occasion of their midnight meal. Unfortunately, though, it is precisely because the boy thus resembled his caregiver and because beings as disparate as even you and I resemble one another, that we ever have any prayer of meeting this constraint amongst ourselves. None of us, though, comes even close to resembling God in this manner. Given our previous strategic admissions when we faced the problem of evil—that morally justifying reasons for God's activities (including deception) may be well beyond our ken—how shall we provide ourselves with any analogous assurance of reliability or trustworthiness in the case involving God's promises? We are not relevantly similar to the source of revelation. We are not well positioned to get good evidence from perception, memory, induction, reason, and the like relevant to a judgment of reliability on the occasion of the Eucharistic meal or God's promises for the afterlife. We are all of us hopeless judges of what is at stake—cosmically speaking—if we are not deceived in some comprehensive, irresistible, and undetectable fashion. Indeed, we are quite utterly in the dark on that matter, as I have been insisting.

Has my worry become salient? Do drink it in. *God is morally permitted to deceive us and for all we know He does deceive us.*

He may have deceived you about what awaits you after death, and He may have deceived me about why I wait in the Garden for His return. Yet my worry worsens; in fact, it explodes. For all any of us knows, He deceives us about a *tremendous* number of topics—from whether there are stars in your sky to whether the blessed incarnation occurred to whether I myself am embodied to whether the sword of flame, the gate, or even the Garden itself exists. That should be disconcerting enough; but given our previous admissions, aren't we utterly in the dark about whether that is exactly what is happening? Unacceptable! Chaotic confusion! There must be a way clear of this insanity!

Why should I fear that my perfectly reasonable belief that starlight shines upon your nights or that I am embodied or that the Garden's gate stands between us is jeopardized by these thoughts? After all, my knowledge of these truths was not acquired by reflecting on those contraband claims about value I humbly relinquished in the discussion of the problem of evil. Surely it was not by calling upon insight that I do not possess into possible goods, possible evils, and the necessary conditions of their realization that I came to know these things, but rather in some independent way, in some way which is not threatened by my ignorance of such abstruse topics as morally justifying reasons or compensating goods, in some way that leaves my other beliefs free of suspicion, well founded, and suitable to guide free choice and action.

And then another hour, another day, another week passes in the Garden and I'm less sure; if we get this far, there may be no turning back. Only temporarily do I breathe a sigh of relief, reminding myself that many of my beliefs are backed independently by appeal to my natural angelic faculties and capacities, by my intuition, memory, perception, introspection, reason, even angelic common sense (for we are gifted that capacity also). But the sense of relief is frail and fleeting as I realize that (again, for all I know) any of my natural faculties and capacities could simply be a divinely selected mechanism that delivers false beliefs, which, although constituting harms to me, nonetheless are permitted by a morally justifying reason that lies beyond my understanding.

It simply won't do merely to inquire—"Is this or that belief of mine grounded in some judgment about possible goods, possible evils, and the necessary conditions of their realization?"—and then to take my confession of ignorance regarding the reasons for God's permitting evils to be a humility-inducing corrective to *Yes* replies, but altogether silent in the case of *No* replies. Nearly all of my beliefs (and yours and those of your kind) are in peril here.

Here is a final way of seeing the difficulty—*in a single thought*: If there really is a morally obligating reason for God to deceive me, then I am deceived, for He always does what He ought. If there is no morally justifying reason for God to deceive me, then I am not deceived, for He never does what He ought not. If there is a morally justifying reason for God to deceive me, then either I am or am not deceived depending on His other purposes. Pitifully, I am utterly in the dark about which of those three antecedent conditions is satisfied. And thus the darkness expands so that I am also utterly in the dark about whether I am deceived in the most comprehensive, irresistible, and undetectable fashion.

I begin to fear that this way lies madness for anyone who accepts that there is a being possessed of nearly unlimited power to deceive and who will use that power when morality demands or when His inscrutable purposes served by doing so do not conflict with what morality demands. What began as a sensible, modest, and well-contained strategy for opposing presumptuous atheistic reasoning from episodes of evil has transformed into a near global catastrophe, threatening to undermine the reasonableness of our views in nearly all matters, great and small.

And I am left with the question of what to do. What is my proper role? Which way do I turn? I cannot doubt His existence, His goodness, His knowledge, or His power—my nature doesn't permit it. I cannot conceive myself His equal even in the absurdly restricted task of understanding the morally justifying reasons for a cyclone or for His hiddenness. I am in the dark about whether my or your massive deception might likewise be an evil which is well compensated for by a good which I can neither recognize as a good nor even have the capacity to entertain should its complexity outrun my representational powers.

These have been my meditations for far too long, and I have been unable to free myself of their force. My thoughts circle through these considerations and convince me only that I wallow in the Garden in irreparable ignorance and that my compliance with His commandments has left me alone and in despair. For ages I have continued, unwavering, in the assurance that my circumstances are not the result of being morally wronged by God, yet other possible scenarios into which I can propel myself certainly possess that minimal and questionable virtue as well. As I asked you before, why should I cooperate with Him and maintain my station in this abyss of unhappiness?

My good is in ruins, and it is all due to *obedience*. Century upon century I've patiently stood—ever ready to play the faithful and devoted sentinel, prepared to contest and repel the unruly horde who would storm the gate and threaten entry of this vacant and God-forsaken place. But, of course, no one approaches or worries the Garden in any way. There is no heroism to furnish matter for poetry on either side of the gate. No one besieges. They don't know I exist.

I have become a fairytale, a myth not to be taken literally, a comical figure in a creation play, an embarrassment to be explained away—a lie. And bereft of any meaningful occupation, I have been reduced to a pathetic voyeur. I waste my substance begging visions from the Tree. I shame myself in not rebelling. I have been a coward for not leaving. Until now.

Since no one will invade my world, I will invade yours.

FIVE

Visions from the Tree

Of course, you must wonder: How could anyone willingly cross such a threshold? What fool would trade the Garden for the fallen world? Well, let me remind you that this play has been performed before and with a cast whose reported reasons and causes were considerably less honorable than my own.

Although not widely recognized, two falls rather than one are depicted in the Holy Story—the fall of man (of your own forebears) and the fall of the rebel angels (of mine)—although historical accident has privileged the first over the second in the theology which has been handed down to you. Both events present puzzles of motivation. How could your ancestors and my kin have left this Garden and the choir of angels, respectively? What could they possibly have lacked that would have even suggested such a course of action in their original and pristine and blessed state, much less that would have recommended it as the favored course to pursue? Was it vanity in Eve, deceit in Adam, pride in the higher angels, lust in the lower? Your kind has speculated for ages. I myself am well acquainted with both story and speculation, but I did not know my brothers' minds, and out of deep respect for them, I reserve judgment on the fall of the angels. Moreover, although I was sole witness to the immediate consequence of the fall of mankind, when I initially beheld the tragic countenance of your first parents, I could not discern any motivation or intention or desire that had directed them in their unhappy choice, and in simple bewilderment I reserve judgment here also.

Whatever the motives behind the falls of our predecessors, as you must now understand from my letter, my own reasons are not born of pride or lust or vanity or sin. Unable to discern whether I am a mere foolish and disposable instrument to be exploited in implementing a divine design, a mute tool possessed of no means by which to discover its genuine purpose or ultimate end—not even through direct (but for all I know) deceitful revelation—I do at least know one truth: I know I am not flourishing. Damaged, I am not yet damned, but neither can I claim any share of happiness.

The question of how to achieve happiness is for us, as it is for you, a momentous one, and in the light (or darkness) of my recent reflections, exactly what constitutes angelic flourishing has become opaque to me. The silence of the Garden presents ample opportunity to repeatedly ask myself—"What makes an angel's existence good for that angel?" A complex question to answer yet such a simple question to ask! Your kind is intimately familiar with the notions of the quality of a life, of a life worth living, of a good life, and you do not hesitate at comparative judgments that some lives go better than others and that some events contribute more to the value of a life than would their absence. Generally it is the same for us, but with a different cause. Ordinarily, the questions occur to you because you see how easily your lives could be better than they are; they occur to the angels because they see how easily their existence could be worse. Here, I am not on the side of the angels.

In asking myself this question, I am not asking after some master list of causes for a life's going well for its subject. I am not asking for a detailed and exhaustive theory of value or even for a comprehensive list of goods. I am not asking for an account of right action, or of virtuous agents, or of praiseworthy subjects—although all of the foregoing questions are to some degree relevant to my theme. I am, instead, asking what things are intrinsically good or bad for a creature of my special kind.

Of course, a great deal then turns on how to type me. I am many things, as are you. You are both a human being and a person. I, too, am a person, but cherub rather than human. Although undoubtedly similar in many ways, my good may differ from yours insofar as I fall under the dominant kind "angelic person" while you must be classed among the sort of person manifested in and thus restricted by a biological animal.

I can begin the process of answering the question relativized to my proper kind by reflecting upon the sorts of items that seem to have direct bearing on my own welfare. Some aspects constitutive of my flourishing surely have to do with the fact that I am embodied strength, fitness, health, beauty. Some emphasize will, proper judgment, or agency—achievement, skill, power, exercise of freedom and autonomy, creativity, contemplation. Some are more passive but nonetheless excellences—joy, experiences of pleasure, aesthetic appreciation. Some an admixture—knowledge and virtue. Lastly, and sadly for me, some are irreducibly social—admiration, respect, friendship, caregiving, mutual love.

Deferring to my previous admission of ignorance regarding compensating goods and morally justifying reasons for the permission of evil, I acknowledge again that I am not in a position to make any all-in claims of value or even of comparative value for this haphazard and almost certainly partial list. But if I know anything at all, I know the social goods here identified are genuine and constitutive of flourishing for the sort of creature I am (even if I cannot fix their ultimate significance in comparison with all the goods there are). And if I don't know anything at all . . . well, then how can I be held accountable for this or that or any other action or belief? No—these are the goods I require. These are the goods I must find the strength and resolution to strive for, even if doing so severs my relation with Him. But what does He care? In His fortress of perfectly permissible silence, He refuses an answer. *Watch.*

I, Tesque, your creation . . . *I call upon you* . . . Speak! Thunder from the air! Rend flesh! Shatter bone! Rain drops of pain! . . . *You coward* . . . Return to see what a mess you have made of this angelic canvas with your fabled artistry! . . . Curse me! Compel me! Forbid me my own sovereignty! . . . *I beg you* . . . Strike me! Crush me! Tear me! Light me! Return me to dust! Hurt me with your presence!

Anything? Anything at all? Nothing at all. *Nothing.*

Why—my daughter—why cooperate with that? Your world of pitch and tar, of hatred and cruelty, of pain and death offers me more, for in the midst of all that suffering I believe I can succeed in my design to act out of love and thereby find some portion of the highest good in creating you and that I can come to feel, however briefly, fellowship with other creatures, to be in the midst of those who will respond to me, to be in some way seen and known.

Honesty requires I admit that the environment I intend to enter upon leaving the Garden is a frightening one. Not that your world poses threats to me (as threats are ordinarily conceived). Nothing can be a danger to me that inhabits your world save the profusion of sin in which I will be invited to partake and in the immediate presence of which even such a one as I may feel tempted from my objective. Earlier I spoke to you of evil, and evil in the form of self-degrading and self-harming sin pollutes your world in greater volume and variety than you could possibly imagine. Yet despite its pervasiveness, its being woven into nearly every thought and word and deed that takes place in your realm, a deep and powerful need for interpersonal love and for penetrating understanding and for personal virtue and for aesthetic excellence wars with sin in even its most significant manifestations. The residual desire for love and for knowledge and for virtue and for beauty in your kind, though dampened and enfeebled by the fall, illuminates even the darkness and despair of sin, and it is that illumination of what you were once and might become again that will make bearable my being amongst you long enough to carry out my intended task.

Permit me to display a few battles in your kind's war with sin. All are historical stories I have witnessed in my evenings at the base of the Tree. Each has made an impact on me as have untold others. Together they lend me courage. Perhaps they will help you understand why choosing to exercise my autonomy and creativity by bringing you into being—even in this desolate house of so many broken and marred lives—seems to be the surest way to achieve and experience flourishing in what will be left of my time before I am punished with annihilation and also to be the method by which to furnish you with the precious gift of existence to do with what you will.

One

For leaving pottery out where it is in danger of being stepped upon and broken, a father from your prehistory strikes his child—much harder than he intended to. Her mother cries out against the act, and, embarrassed at his loss of control, he raises his hand menacingly at her in turn, but with no chance of carrying through as they both well know. His irritability has never been so high; anything triggers it. He cannot shake his experience with the other men. He glowers and to himself muses—I was in the right, after all, and they wouldn't admit it! I had persuasively argued that just as no one thinks this year's snow is last year's snow or this moon's rain last moon's rain or the grass of this Spring the grass of seasons past, no one should think that the sun that rises tomorrow in the east is the sun that will set tonight in the west. Nature's cycles prove it. There is, of course, a great succession of suns, one sparked anew each morning, blazing at the noon, dimming at the horizon, spent as it dips from sight, finally allowing night to reign until his brother is born and crosses the sky on the morrow. Those fools who insist that there is but one sun madly racing under the ground to get back to its origin before the night is over, mysteriously replenishing its store of whatever oil it burns along the way . . . what are they thinking? They insult the God of the sun and diminish his creations, making him out to be some imbecilic child who uses the same cup every day. They try to invoke the moon, but . . . well, that's a different story altogether. They just won't listen to reason. It's so unjust.

And so the disgruntled father lashes out in fevered wrath, but his love is ultimately for justice and for proper acknowledgment and admiration of his reasoning (which, although mistaken in its conclusions, has something in its favor). His love has been perverted in anger and tinged with a desire for revenge, but its genuine objects are fine.

Two

Long past his prime, past even his predicted death, the second oldest man in the tribe arrives early to watch the girls dance. Fixated, the matrons watch the watching. He should be ashamed, they declare one to another. Open mouthed and ogling. Wrinkled and staggering. It's disgusting. What does he think he could possibly do with one of them? It's appalling. His body is failing, but his hearing is not. Cut by their remarks, he struggles to stand and departs. But there is an answer to their question. He could look at the girls for hours, fondly and sadly in turns, recalling his own youth, his virility, his physical power, his departed magnificence of body. Time is no one's ally in old age, and decades have carved heavy ribbons into his flesh and brittled his bones, but his sexual cravings have lingered. No longer desirable, he desires all the more. He wishes to touch and to caress and to kiss and to please the dancing bodies. To experience once more the closeness with another that is celebrated in shared sexual intimacy. Somehow, however, these desires are not recognized for what they are, and an indiscriminate hunger for visual access to the youthful female form, to any youthful female form, to interchangeable parts on display, has taken their place. Humiliated, he is later discovered by the matrons stealing further glances from behind a tent, a hand under his cloth.

And so the elder is caught out in a premeditated moment of self-emptying lasciviousness, but his love is truly directed at strength, fitness, health, beauty, sexual goods, union, and intimacy with another. His love has been perverted in lust, but its genuine objects are noble.

Three

The barn is cold. The yard is cold. The house is cold. Everything cold. Why—whispers the servant whose livelihood depends entirely on the whim of her employer—why do I have to rouse myself before dawn to burden and chore, while my mistress sleeps the sleep of the coddled? Yelling at me for not having the fire at full flame before six? Demanding this? Commanding that? She is no more deserving than I am. She was given her wealth, her position, her power. Such arrogance in one who has earned nothing! If anything, our places should be exchanged; my labor rewarded, her uselessness punished by slaving for and answering to me. Everyone should start the race at the same line. We all have seen the moon—no significant difference separates us. Only time and chance. I would rob her of it all, even if I could not take her place.

Audible misery, but this isn't the petulant whining of one bested in a contest of merit, that all-too-familiar mother of jealous speech and thought; rather it is the lament of one who loves fairness in distribution of goods and disdains lopsided privilege that bestows unearned benefits on one as it levels undeserved harms on another. Her love has been perverted in envy, but its genuine objects are admirable.

Four

Everyone, everywhere, everywhen, cries out—vanity of vanity, all is vanity. All is transitory, directionless, purposeless, without value. No accomplishment endures. No character changes. Nothing compels. All is vanity.

A literary scholar—your contemporary—rocks at his desk in self-congratulatory delight upon completing a manuscript illuminating the political commitments of a great poem. But time blinks and no one studies the manuscript, another blink and no one remembers the poem, another blink and the profusion of literary texts is so expansive no one can read a trillionth of it all.

Your scholar reflects—if his kind survives another billion years, nearly two hundred thousand periods of time each equal to the period of time during which all current literature has been composed will elapse. The world's present literary output will then be to the whole as a single letter on a page is to a modern novel. Whence literature? A great unreadable and uncategorizable mountain of unheard songs and unappreciated tales. Why—asks the scholar, his giddiness departed—why squander any effort, resource, or passion contributing leaves to such a mute and useless compost pile?

In any of its endless disguises this is perhaps the most dangerous battle to engage with sin, for confrontation with sloth exposes not so much a disordered love as love defeated and extinguished. Redirecting love toward its proper objects cannot be accomplished unless that mislaid love is again taken up and rekindled. Yet so frequently do seemingly emptied souls with no visible well of support miraculously lift themselves from despondency and resolutely stumble once again in the direction of the good! Sans guarantee, sans sustaining belief, sans motivating desire . . . their bare faith pushes them forward.

Five

A composer retreats from the music into the bottle. The audience applauds the superb performance of the first act of his opera, but absorbed in meticulously critiquing the sauces on the beef set before him, he slumps in the composer's box, deaf to the appreciation of his artistry, and worries a fifth glass of wine. Obsessed with the presentation of the meal, he rejects it a third time, demanding that the chef meet his impossible expectations. In drink, he takes too much, too soon, too ravenously, and spends excessively in pursuit of tastes he cannot distinguish. In food, he barely manages to meet his basic nutritional needs, for no quantity, no quality, no arrangement, no temperature, no seasoning, no admixture is satisfactory. In both, unnatural and disproportionate concern with what he sees, smells, tastes, and ingests crowds out everything else worthy of attention, starves his relationships, and diminishes even the music with which he has been so richly gifted. Month after month, however, he recognizes and abhors his addiction and his pettiness. Vowing to reform once and for all, he is stone drunk within a fortnight, trading the integrity of his body and squandering his talent for pleasures of the palate that no longer ever materialize. Tomorrow he will look in the mirror and swear off his addiction again.

And so this shackled composer fusses over and spoils every meal and slakes his every thirst, but his love primarily aims at the aesthetic appreciation of the sights, sounds, odors, tastes, and textures of his environment. His love has been perverted in a gluttony that alienates without gratifying, but its genuine objects are wondrous.

Six

"The most generous woman they have ever known. She would give away her last dollar, share her meal with a stranger, offer her finest scarf to a shivering waif." The professor has always delighted in such descriptions and has worked hard to make them true. She has made herself a woman who knows the worth of worldly possessions and that their value nearly always consists in their ability to be bestowed on others in need of them. She lives a Spartan life with iron will-power, free of the disease of acquisition, indifferent to the pressures of advertising, proud of and contented in her simplicity. Never shy or apologetic about taking a share large enough to satisfy her meagre and reasonable needs, she has enough . . . in all areas but one, for she is a knowledge miser. Head and shoulders above her peers in her astounding collection of facts, theories, interconnections, concrete know-how, and abstract speculation, she aches for more. More history, more philosophy, more literature, more religion, more physics,

64

more mathematics, more . . . detail. She will select an article for which she has but a passing interest over a tea party with her child, an outdated documentary that promises a tidbit or two of trivia over intimacy with her husband, any opportunity to increase her stockpile of data at almost any expense. Fanatical pursuit of information drives her moral decision-making, often in the wrong direction. If there were only a way to make a gift of one's knowledge at the expense of not retaining it oneself, she would see exactly how little claim she has to the title of generosity that so many of her family and friends bestow upon her. She does not care for dollars, meals, or scarves; parting from them is nothing to her. But ask her to relinquish some hard-won understanding in exchange for a substantial benefit distributed to those she most loves and watch the panic that ensues, behold the excuses that are devised, witness a selfishness that prefers to augment a good which is already plentifully enjoyed at the expense of real suffering to herself and others.

And so the self-deceived professor compliments herself on her capacity to withstand the multifaceted temptation of greed while being as tightly bound by that sin as anyone ever caught in its grip, but her love aspires to knowledge and to deep understanding of herself and her relation to the world. Her love has been perverted in avarice, but its genuine objects are splendid.

Six brief sketches of your busy world, six fleeting glances at my projected home. The light glimpsed in these contests of virtue and vice I have witnessed and have here painted for you in words is nearly overwhelmed by the darkness of sin, yet this inadequate and faint light is a greater good than the inexhaustible and deplorable sin is an evil. I am able and prepared to accept the balance. I am willing to leave the Garden for such a world to make my attempt, even if only for a short while, to number among its lights.

As with all creatures, an angel's life can be good or bad for its subject, and as with your kind, my good consists in a variety of physical forms, mental states, intellectual, moral, and creative activities, and social excellences. Many of these components I enjoy in abundance, but in the last and most important category—where reside interpersonal interaction and mutual love—I have been intentionally deprived. Know that I am not wrong in this judgment, naïvely mistaking dislike for disvalue, for the very first negative evaluation to appear in the Holy Story proves He thinks so, too. Immediately upon placing Adam in the Garden, God said,

> It is not good that the man should be alone; I will make him an help meet for him.

Mere moments to be endured before his precious and favored pet was blessed with companion, because being alone was not good! *It is outrageous.*

Millennia have passed for me—during which I have learned and relearned and learned again that it is not good for any sentient creature to remain alone. He knows this and nevertheless has marooned me to suffer in His absence and my seclusion. Why have I been allowed no companion to soften or render bearable my exile, no friend or second self with whom to share the joys of union and of love freely given and received, not even a dog, for which I would suffer all the privations of the Garden? I have been permitted only mathematics and the Tree, and neither speaks.

His cruelty releases me of my service; His indifference removes my obligation. I will quit this post and seek my own companions. I shall follow in the steps of the lost angels, turn from God, disobey. And before I am forever exorcised from this world, I shall take upon myself the performance of at least one creative act that has not been decreed and prescribed by the One who has forsaken me and has become indifferent to my good.

You shall be its issue.

Obedience or Rebellion?

Another morning bathes the Garden in light, and I am still here. The gate remains closed. Today I begin a new cycle of the naming of the twelve animals in my afternoon river walks. I am a coward for not leaving.

I have been studying my letter to you, daughter, and I hesitate. How can it be that on such mixed and fragile foundations I contemplate vacating the Garden to unite with a mere human animal? Certainly, no equal awaits seduction in your world below, and I fear I may not be alluring to your kind, for all angels are terrifying, even those who approach in love. Yet, I hope to follow a pedigreed precedent. You are familiar with this passage in the Holy Story?

> And it came to pass, when men began to multiply on the face of the earth, and daughters were born unto them, that the sons of God saw the daughters of men that they were fair; and they took them wives of all which they chose . . . and also after that, when the sons of God came in unto the daughters of men, and they bare children to them, the same became mighty men which were of old, men of renown.

Such were the exploits of my fallen brothers; such the reputations of your ancestral cousins.

I have already done my best to describe what I hope to achieve by my joining your masquerade below: I would abandon this uncertain Garden to participate in something I know to be good and fine, thereby momentarily flourish, and finally fade into nonbeing. And you, undamaged and pure, so freshly equipped with opportunities and potential I no longer can claim to possess, would replace me in the world, perhaps to be someday completed in union with He who has discarded me. I may hope for you what has been denied to me, and I can initiate that possibility while enriching what remains of my tattered but angelic being.

But—I must ask—what do I and what do others stand to lose with this choice? I pardon my continuing presence in the Garden with an attempt to address myself to this last theme.

One other in particular—whoever will contribute the other half of your being—may well suffer some unforeseen injustice as a result of my peculiar inexperience with others, despite all my efforts to minimize the complications that must arise from the union of two such unequal creatures. Does that sound vulgar? Harsh? Cruel? Unacceptably indifferent to the good of another? One thought: A life of perfectly proper action, a life without moral wrongdoing, may yet fail to be a flourishing or a virtuous life. And the flourishing life, a life brimming over with goodness for its subject, may contain some number of impermissible deeds, foreseen or otherwise. Possibly, flourishing and right action can walk together never out of step, as can withering and misdeed, but it is a happy coincidence when they do. Flourishing and right action can also take separate paths when an unobliging environment forces them in different directions, as has mine. The moment of choice is perilous. Ask not which you *ought* to select (for that phrasing of the question is loaded in favor of right action) and ask not which is *better for you* (for that manner of inquiring favors flourishing). Ask instead which you *prefer*. One of your depths will thereby be revealed. Perhaps foretelling my fall, I have surprised myself in discovering that when forced to choose I number among those who prefer flourishing to sinlessness.

Thus it remains to ponder the question of harms to myself. What do *I* risk losing in this venture? Earlier I spoke of annihilation, of eventually trespassing in my disobedience some forbidden threshold and softly vanishing away as would anything released by the divine hand and no longer attended to by the divine mind. But now it is time for us to confront and to speak honestly of the alternative.

The evidence to be gained from examining the fates of those souls who have fallen before me, evidence relevant to forecasting the likelihood of my success in carrying out my design, distresses to the point of despair. The absolute and utter change which befell my brothers, the rebellious angels, is *astonishing*. Such blessed and beautiful purity freely transforming itself into crippled and permanent corruption is perhaps the worst event ever to have transpired. If their choice is in fact irrevocable and the atonement is not extended to them (and, I must add, the Holy Story is true rather than a deception in league with the impenetrable divine plan), then they have made the worst mistake it is possible to make. They have traded eternal happiness for self-elected agony and hopelessness without end. But then I remind myself of my reasons for considering my own, my personal, rebellion. Mine are not the incentives of pride and lust, as the rumors which so tarnished the reputations of my unfortunate brothers reported theirs to be. My motivation is not to satisfy some self-absorbed and base desire, but an attempt to seek my own flourishing and your good, in the least destructive way I know how. Doing so requires my disobedience, yes . . . but for the reasons I have cataloged earlier, obedience cannot justly be required of me given my inability to acquire any reasonable belief from the promises and revelations of our hidden Father who may (for all we know) be a Father of Lies, albeit a perfectly good and perfectly loving one.

If I fall while beguiled by such noble thoughts and with such honorable and value-directed purpose, could I really be punished by transforming in the same hideous way? Could a nature as superb as my own possibly be stretched that far? Haven't my fallen brothers somehow brought this ruin upon themselves with improper motives, concealed thoughts, malicious desires, and secret vices that are opaque to me now but that I will have the strength to resist should I also eventually come within their influence?

Ah, but why do I so arrogantly flirt with conceptions of myself as possessed of an integrity of character and a strength of will that those above me in the hierarchy did not possess or else could not maintain post-rebellion? What if I am radically mistaken? What if this splendid portrait I so vigorously paint of myself is nothing like its disfigured, complacent, and self-deceived subject? What if I do not know my own mind—a mind unveiled only after the Garden's gate locks behind me—and I watch in horror as who I have chosen to become bursts into your world as only another misguided and loathsome miscreant, another instrument for evil with power, opportunity, and nothing left to lose?

This last is the question that torpefies me, fills me with doubt, ridicules my strategies, and rivets my attention upon your kind rather than my own to better understand the consequences of rebellion when it is predicated on reasons that—if in fact I have not been entirely honest in my self-description and am poisoned by duplicity and vanity—may be closer to my own. What changes in one's nature attend one's initial disobedience of God and subsequently pressure if not determine one's future course of action?

Your first parents were perfect specimens of your kind—dust, yet possessed of tremendous intellects, disciplined-but-free wills, finely crafted bodies, and well-ordered desires all enclosed in a paradisiacal environment where they were preserved from decay, safe from evil and death, and equipped with both a range of preternatural gifts and precisely attuned natural attitudes in harmony with the value of the objects in their surroundings.

I—superior dust—in my currently unfallen and unspoiled state, similarly represent the best of my kind, and I, too (momentarily setting aside my worries of divine deception), apparently reside in a state of innocence and protection in this pristine Garden, immune from whatever lies beyond its gate, naturally invested with the right attitudes toward the right objects in the right proportions. I, too, appear to be an agent fully furnished with the power of significant freedom, in particular, the power not to succumb to sin. Perhaps my high ideals, my fervent sense of an incorruptible self, my fierce confidence in single-mindedly pursuing my objective outside the Garden arises only because I am currently safely ensconced within its walls and bolstered by a supernatural grace reserved for the obedient.

For what happened to that happy couple so superbly prepared and fitted for eternity in the Garden? Upon my waking to first consciousness, hearing of their transgression and the pronouncement of their heavy sentence, accepting my charge to be its executor, and turning them out of doors, the devastating effects of their fall emerged immediately and without interruption or mercy.

Your own theologians have disagreed on the proper characterization of these consequences, but that the change was severe is uniformly conceded across all variations. The more lenient theorists claim that their preternatural gifts were withdrawn in accordance with their loss of station, but that theirs was simply a fall from a state of supernatural grace to a natural state—a state characterized by a reign of concupiscence, that persistence of disordered desire which, as the source of all future sins, maintains its subjects in a state of alienation from God. But still, it is possible to view such loss as a penalty of privation rather than a positive impairment of the human nature. The less lenient theorists instead claim that this state of concupiscence (and of ignorance, pain, and subjection to death) is a kind of disease or corruption that amounts to a wounded and perverted nature—to a punishing impairment rather than a gift rescinded.

I side with the less lenient. Having spent all my evenings observing every corner of your world through the window of the Tree . . . far more than a mere privation, far more than an assortment of dangers threatening frail human nature unshielded by the armor of divine grace, I have detected a more horrific outcome still, for there have I seen and tasted the appalling fruits of a nearly entirely corrupted and wrecked human nature—an abysmal state of depravity that I can scarcely bear to consider.

Is that to be my fate, as well?

Of course, I fully accept that in exiting this divinely illuminated

Garden I am certain to experience, to some degree, the double darkness of sin and ignorance. But do I hazard acquiring a nearly completely corrupted and wrecked angelic nature, as well? Am I on the verge of willing myself into an abyss of misery from which I can never return? For I fear that perhaps unlike your first parents and their progeny, my punishment will not be a near, but rather a total, depravity. As you know from my retelling of the visions from the Tree, I believe it is possible for your kind to war against your depraved natures, to be conflicted but occasional, if inconstant, lights in the battle with sin, but perhaps only the human nature is spared depravity entire. If the Holy Story is true, fallen man may be redeemed by way of atonement. Fallen angels may simply become demons lost.

For all my desire to do and to experience good . . . would that be my fate, as well?

Is this inexplicable obedience—which, I repeat in vexation, cannot be known to be my highest purpose, even if I know He who tells me so to be perfectly good and perfectly loving—is this eternity of cooperation in wretched isolation and deafening divine silence so priceless that my seeking our joint good, daughter, will be rewarded by the unalterable spoiling of my angelic nature? So much more terrible than quick and unexplained annihilation would be the thwarting of my heart's desire by my own fallen and demonic will!

But then, what of you? If I do not leave this Garden, you do not exist. What is your counsel? Risk all or remain? O that you could answer! And so once again . . . I reread my remarks, rehearse my reasons, revisit my reservations . . . and stand paralyzed as another night descends on Paradise.

I continue to frighten myself, and I have not yet faced the worst. I sing the sorrow of annihilation or worldly corruption, but even greater misfortune threatens. What of *judgment* and thereafter? If annihilated, I have nothing to fear at the great judgment (but also nothingness to fear). If preserved, then after a brief sojourn in your world, whether succeeding in giving rise to you or falling into degeneracy and failure, I will be consigned. But where?

Would He, acting out of perfect justice, reject me—thus ensuring I receive whatever I deserve? Or would He, acting out of perfect love, instead accept my choice to reject Him—a choice I will be in danger of enacting should I become enveloped in sin?

If Hell is conceived as punishment, and I make myself of damnable character, then won't His justice constrain Him to submit me to it? If Hell is no punishment but rather an elected state, and in foolishness and iniquity I so choose, then won't I end there all the same? And *nothing* can prepare a mind to contemplate such an eternal fate. Choose any interval, the longest you can fathom. Take it to its own power, take that to its own power, and let the result be your base unit of time. Survive any number of those units and you are no closer to completing your season in Hell than you will ever be. As I said before, every finite number is small. Torment is unnecessary. Alienation and separation will suffice. Eternity in any state short of blissful and perfect mutual love will become an unbearable agony which nonetheless must somehow be borne.

Yet, maddeningly, the risk of the infinite disvalue of never-ending damnation does not immediately speak in favor of remaining in the Garden. I cannot pretend my earlier reflections on divine deception were without force. And as they taught me, for all I know, faithfulness at my post risks infinite disvalue as well, as does any alternative open to me. Risk is unavoidable, no decision safe. If I am a ship's dog—perfectly loved—but only to the proper threshold at which my well-being becomes negotiable in securing greater goods, then cooperation and obedience in the Garden may be the one option unsurpassable in disvalue for me.

Of course, I could trust that, acting out of perfect mercy and grace, He would welcome me, celebrate my return, redeem me and my fallen brothers as He redeems all creation. I could hope for universal salvation—no matter in what mistaken direction my will has wandered. But any such hope would be blind. His perfect goodness and perfect love require that He desires such a universal reconciliation and perhaps even that He would ensure it should it not conflict with higher goods (or should it not entail hidden, unacceptable evils). Yes—and are those all-important conditions satisfied? Unknown and unknowable for you and me.

How can His forgiveness for any choice of mine not be mandatory? The question rings out again and again in my mind with such overpowering force! My decision to leave or to stay will be a product of my beliefs, desires, and character, but they are *mine* only in the sense of correctly characterizing me . . . my beliefs and desires are not under my voluntary control. If they were, I would have long since brought this ache of loneliness to an end in a triumphant act of will. My unfortunate character was chosen but not by me. I am jeopardized by my nature, but it has been imposed on me from without by my Creator who thought it proper to invest this angelic dust with mechanisms that not only cause it anguish but overwhelmingly incline it to seek its own good by rushing from safety and grace to oblivion or worse. How can His forgiveness not be mandatory?

Tomorrow I will choose.

A final thought to help me on my way to you. In the form of a story. Not entirely from the Tree.

Forever ago . . . a man and woman stood where I stand. Each perfectly planted in Paradise, yet each destined to depart this blessed Garden, to leave this Sanctuary, never to return.

Beguiled? Deceived? Dissatisfied? Arrogant? Proud? Lustful? Searching . . . for power? Liberation? Knowledge? Or was it simply a *declining*—a free and voluntary relinquishing of all the good in the world on the grounds that obedience (even to a single inconsequential rule) was too crushing a price—from a couple who would be Gods themselves? Gods without the power to provide themselves a single instant of happiness; Gods without the wisdom to foresee what they were choosing.

And yet despite their flinging in His face all the gifts they had received, including the most precious gift of their own being and their own place in creation, the Holy Story offers a promise of atonement and redemption for these creatures that have freely made such wretches of themselves. They graciously receive a second opportunity. Moreover, a staggering number of others receive a first opportunity, an opportunity that would not have been theirs were it not for the missteps of their first parents. *O fortunate fault!*

Take away the primal sin, and everyone born into your world after the expulsion from the Garden is swept away as well. Cain did not pre-exist his birth, an immaterial soul patiently awaiting access to an animal body furnished by the copulation of his parents. Cain, a man of dust, *is* identical to that body, the very body which (if the Holy Story is true) will rise renewed with all others on the day of resurrection and judgment. And as with Cain, so with you all. None of you would be elements in the cosmos, characters in this great creation play, participants in the free co-creation of the world with God, had I not hurled your ancestors from this sacred Garden into the land of Nod. *O happy sin!*

Adam himself wondered whether his fall would precipitate a more splendid and sublime world than could have been actualized in the absence of sin and absent the magnificent goods of incarnation and atonement. Many times he asked in prayer whether he should rejoice that his error in judgment or that his weakness of will would eventually bring forth goods greater than any that could have attended a sinless eternity in the Garden—a prayer in response to which our silent Father has yet to supply an answer to him or to anyone.

Yet even if the answer to that question is beyond our capacities, daughter, and we cannot together sing *O Felix Culpa* in confident knowledge that the goods of a fallen world outstrip those of an unfallen one, your kind can and should recognize that the fall of man at least has the joyful consequence of providing them with life and with the opportunity to find an eternal place at the Lord's table.

And, thus, my daughter, you may similarly come to regard *my* fall—should all my justifications come to nothing and should I, too, be about to embark upon a fool's errand—you may come to regard my fall as a fortunate fault, a happy sin, for it will at least have led to you.

I cannot continue to delay. Tomorrow I will choose.

Tomorrow came. The morning light illuminated all the brilliant colors of the Garden. The river ran.

For the first time since the banishing of its original inhabitants, Tesque lifted the flaming sword from its place in the ground, inserted that peculiar key into the great lock of the Garden's gate, and gently opened the door to Paradise.

Forever, it would seem, he stood motionless while the wind rustled the leaves of the two trees at his back.

PART II

JOY

SEVEN

A Beast Sings

I also walk in the Garden. Tesque and I began here on the same day. He is my friend.

I don't know you, but you seem to be a friend of Tesque's, too. He talks to you often, but I can't tell where you are or how you hear him. I thought I might try talking to you too, then maybe I will be able to see you, and you can join us in the Garden.

I think it would be good if you came to visit us. Tesque is sad. He is sad about a lot of things and most of the time. There is a lot to not be sad about, though. We have a morning walk each day. The flowers are beautiful. The grass is beautiful. The trees are beautiful. The smells are indescribable! I am a dog, and that's important to me. Tesque is beautiful. I am beautiful, too, but Tesque doesn't see me. I've tried many different things to get his attention, but he's always too busy with his thoughts. I mean he really doesn't see me. I don't think he knows I'm here. I know it, though. I wish he did. I wonder why he doesn't. I wonder whether he would recognize me as his friend, if he saw me.

Hard thoughts are important. I'm pretty sure about that. But I'm also pretty sure that Tesque thinks they are more important than they really are. That's why he always chooses them over all the other things that are good, too. He misses out. I have a much better time on our morning walks. I investigate everything, and I see and hear and smell and taste and touch all the little changes in the Garden that he doesn't detect. He's really good at examining the very same things and coming to master them, but he looks at so very few of the available things to look at. Tesque is much stronger and ever so much smarter than me, and I admire that. But it hasn't made him any happier. He likes to say (in a really deep voice) "I am made of superior dust" and "I am the guard dog of dust." I don't know who he says it to, but it comforts him. I don't think he's right, though. I don't think he should be assigned to watch over anything. He's not very good at it. He only notices what he wants to. In fact, I have to watch over him so that habit of his won't get him into trouble. I'm always ready to help him if I can. In fact, *I* am the guard dog of dust! (Laughter) *I* am the guard dog of dust!

Tesque is mad that his name didn't show up in his special story. At least he has a name. I didn't have one at all. But I decided I wanted one, and so I gave myself one. A nice name. From one of Tesque's stories that he tells aloud. It was pretty easy to do. I am Lazaraistones.

In the afternoons we always splash in the river. It's my favorite time of day. I love the water. I love how the light reflects off its surface, its coldness, its taste, and just how much Tesque enjoys it. He doesn't admit it, but I think it's his favorite time of day, too. I can tell that he especially likes the rush of the water against him. I think he imagines that the water is playing with him.

I leave the river before he does. He wants to chant his names. I don't get it. It's probably important because he never forgets to do it, but it's not something I can do with him. I don't know what my part is. Instead, I always spend later afternoons with the Tree. The Tree is very kind. I eat the fruit that falls from his branches, and we always talk about a lot of wonderful things. And the Tree shows me pictures and sounds that aren't in the Garden. We laugh and have fun with that together. We talk about the pictures, and the Tree helps me understand them. The Tree is really strong and smart like Tesque, but the Tree isn't sad. The Tree doesn't need as much from me as Tesque does. That's why I always curl up against Tesque instead of the Tree when he comes to join us in the evenings. I think it helps Tesque because even though he doesn't see me, he leans on me. He's really heavy, but it doesn't matter. I can take it. I am made of superior dust, too!

The Tree shows different pictures and sounds to Tesque—the ones he wants to see. Tesque and the Tree don't talk about the pictures or understand them together; they just watch. I don't enjoy those as much. I nap.

Tesque is mad about the pictures. He is mad at God about the pictures. He thinks God should help the people in the pictures and then spend time with them. I think maybe God does. Tesque doesn't think so. I don't know. I don't think Tesque knows either.

I wonder a lot about something I heard Tesque say—that none of us can be friends with God. I admit I don't ever see God either. But I see his Garden and all the splendid things it contains. And I see Tesque and the Tree. And I see myself (well most of myself). And those things are pretty good. And God gave them to me. Or gave me to them. Or gave us all to each other. I love God for that.

Sometimes Tesque talks and even shouts right into the air. It's the way he thinks aloud about his hard topics. I like it when he does that because I can sit right in front of him and pretend he is shouting directly to me. Tesque has some very strange, hard thoughts. He thinks God might hurt us and then lie about it. Sort of. Maybe he doesn't think it, but he worries about it a lot. I've listened to his reasons when I'm pretending he is talking to me. They are too hard for me. The reasons are pretty interesting, though. I don't know what's wrong with them, but I am not convinced by them. I suspect I should probably worry more about it, too.

Tesque has been talking more and more frequently about leaving the Garden to get you. You would be welcome here. It would be such a delight to share the Garden with you and Tesque. We could walk together and splash together and watch pictures together and be together.

But to tell you the truth, friend, I'm scared. I'll miss him terribly if he goes on an errand like that. What if he never came back? I wouldn't know how to find him, and I can't imagine what the Garden would be without him.

I don't want him to leave. Perhaps there is some way I can help him? He writes down those things he says aloud. Maybe I could bring those words to you on their papers, and then you could see why it would be good if you came to visit us. And Tesque would stay safe. I'll ask the Tree if he knows where you are.

⊂⊃⊂⊃

The Tree and I have talked. He didn't make the scared feelings go away, but he let me explain them for a long time, and he felt them with me. The Tree is a good listener. The Tree seemed worried about Tesque, too, and explained that what Tesque has written to you is a letter. He said that this is Tesque's way of talking himself into something. The Tree said he was sorry but that I am not able to help Tesque by taking his letter to you (but I didn't understand why). The Tree also told me that he is aware of someone else who might very much benefit from reading Tesque's letter (although it wasn't really written to her) and that there is some chance I might be able to help her instead, if I am willing. He said that she is having difficulties that are similar to Tesque's but different.

I don't really know anything else about her except that she is in trouble in a way that concerns the Tree and that I might have the power to help her. That's enough information for me. I'd like to try.

The Tree told me how I can find her, but I'll have to leave the Garden for a little while. I've never thought of doing that before. Tesque won't notice, and I do want to be a friend to her, whether I succeed in helping or not. Then maybe you and her, Tesque and I, and the Tree can someday all be together, too. There is room in the Garden for all of us.

PART III

NAPHIL

EIGHT

A Night Visitor

Entry One

OK—so let's pretend. Three times I've tried to start this diary over the last ten days, and three times I've produced only kindling paper for the next morning's fire. What's wrong with me? I am sickeningly self-conscious and overly concerned with my appearance—at least with the appearance of my thoughts, for who could be concerned with the appearance of *this* body? "I shall write for myself"—I repeatedly vow—and within a paragraph I'm fantasizing over who might stumble upon my words. I immediately desire their approval, and to some invisible audience, staring over my shoulder on the verge of applause, I address myself, disguise myself, and thwart whatever purpose this stupid, private journal was supposed to serve. But why? In general, I can't stand an audience. Or a crowd. Even a crowd of two. But if I can't write to me, then let me write to an imaginary friend. God knows I don't have a real one. It's a better arrangement.

"Dear Friend"—no. "Dear Tesque"—no.

"Dear *Father*"—yes, let's go with that conceit! Delightful. Dear *father*, I received your "letter" three nights ago under rather bizarre circumstances. I'm still not used to this house. My retreat began here a week ago on Midsummer's Day, and a structure this old—made out of wood and earth and moss and stone and held upright by the wind—makes noises unlike any I've ever heard. Enough to make you think the place was haunted, if you believe in that sort of thing. Well, I don't, but I was jarred awake anyway—the gate to the yard clattering back and forth—and, unable to return to sleep, I half groped my way out to the fireplace to find enough gin and tonic for a midnight snack. That's when I happened into my little friend who's curled up against me now. I can't believe the owner of this property would have been so careless as to leave such a loving bundle behind. But then again, like everyone else in this dismal, frozen, rustic corner of the world, he didn't seem tremendously competent when I was finalizing arrangements to rent the house. The breed is hard to fix—some sort of terrier perhaps—but he's larger than any terrier I've ever seen. Denser, too, if that's the right word. He's healthy enough, but I've no idea what he could have been eating for most of the past week or how he's been sneaking in and out to do his business. No traces. I chose this place for its remoteness, and he's far too clean to have arrived from any distance on foot; so I suppose he really must have been tucked away somewhere in here all along.

I certainly harbored no desire for company, but I'd be lying if I denied that I'm happy to have found him. He's hilarious. As you could imagine, I was rather taken aback to encounter a dog, but I can't say he appeared very startled to discover me. If anything, he seemed surprised that I noticed him at all. For an hour or so he darted about the room, and each time my eyes would follow him or I would speak to him, he wagged his whole body so forcefully I thought he would fall over. And when he barks it sounds like *laughter*. It's infectious! The first time I've laughed, I mean really laughed, in . . . well, I can't remember how long.

No ribbons, no collar, no tags? Irresponsible, but unsurprising. One way or another I suspect he'll be coming with me when I quit this house. Even if I have to sneak out a day or two early and settle up final rental accounts by mail. Whoever abandoned him here surely doesn't deserve him. Besides—I've never fallen for any living thing so fast and so completely as I have for this wonderful little guy. Who would have thought a solitude-retreat could be so enhanced just for the presence of a dog? Would that the whole world were populated with canines! If there were a button for that, I'd push it in a heartbeat.

Who am I kidding? Enhanced? Barely salvaged, rather. It was a serious mistake to come all the way out here without better preparation to make more profitable use of my time alone. Enchanting, of course, to be free of dreadful interaction with other people, but without a plan, without the distraction of work to plow through, I just have myself. And it hasn't taken me very long to remember— I don't like myself. My one chance to finally get away from others mishandled, and then what? I would have either skulked back early and in defeat or (if I could find bravery enough) the alternative. What a blessing—this dog. And I'd been assuming I'd saved him.

If we're going to spend all this time together, I suppose he'll need a name. I haven't done much right lately, but I can hardly get this one wrong. I'll call him Joy.

Entry Two

So, *father*, quite a wild story you've got there. I should mention that Joy found it—not me. I kept my promise to stay out of the study where the owner of the hovel keeps his private this and thats, but Joy apparently didn't make any such promise and was happily chewing on it when I discovered him. In fact, I'm pretty sure he must have been hunkered down in the study for the first several days of my turn here at the house. The wind has disclosed a partially concealed hole in the wall behind the desk just large enough for him to squeeze himself back and forth into the yard, and with all this Icelandic rain there was no shortage of water to drink. His source of food and his utter cleanliness are still mysteries, though.

Still—*quite a story*—and all in longhand, without errors, and in perfectly uniform script. Good God, that kind of precision must have taken forever! I can't write a page without two dozen scratch outs and words running up the margins when I've exhausted all the revising room. But seriously, I trust neither the nearly illiterate caretaker of the house nor any of the dimwitted laborers in the village and surrounding farms had much to do with its authorship. And, pretense aside, *you* didn't write it, *Tesque*. So, what business could that simpleton have with a perfectly hand-lettered, heavy-ink manuscript on what looks like pretty artsy-craftsy paper? It's just so wildly out of place here.

Entry Three

Well, *father*, I must say your origin is something of a mystery, since I can't find any traces of authorship or publication on the web. Mulling over your story has been my sole occupation for the last several days. Really, it's all I've done; I've scarcely eaten or ventured outside, and I've certainly not been able to focus my attention on any of my own misconceived and malformed projects. Joy never lets me out of his sight and seems most content when I'm engrossed in the letter. *The letter.* It's nagging and gnawing at me. I feel a tangible compulsion to address this experience. Confront its bizarre and provocative content head on. Debate its protagonist. Deal with these ludicrous thoughts before they get any further out of hand. At first blush, I judged it little more than a curious and entertaining narrative—intellectually challenging, character-driven, preachy at times but engrossing, off-beat, melancholy, supernatural—just my style, but that's not it. That's not it at all. It's *creepy*. I can't let it alone. A mood has settled. I can't shake the impression that the letter is intended for and written expressly to me. Stupid, I know.

But I'm not thinking just of the coincidences. Anyone adopted without a backstory naturally wonders about her real parents. I'm no exception. When I was little—well, I suppose this body was never *little*—but when I was younger, I would imagine my real father suddenly arriving unannounced and alone, in fancy dress and exotic skin tone, handsome, powerful, forcing his way through some weedy barricade erected by my loathsome adoptive parents in order to find and carry me away. I have to admit, though, my imaginary father never swept in to free me from my childhood prison in the glimmering robes of an angel! Or in the tattered robes of a demon for that matter. It's not that I'm dead set against believing in such beings, although I can't really say I wholeheartedly do. If pressed, I suspect I would defer to my religious tradition which unambiguously teaches there most assuredly are such creatures out and about somewhere or other, busily engaged in their sacred or nefarious work. *Genuine* Christianity, I mean—not the milquetoast, intellectually skittish, sycophantic, run-from-tradition, stuttering, panic-in-the-presence-of-science, impoverished, apologize-for-your-doctrines, near-atheism that goes by the name of Christianity, even in the mouths of some powerful bishops. It's just that if such things populate the world, I'll wager they have precious little to do with the likes of me, and it just never occurred to me to exercise my imagination in that particular fashion. An *angel* of all things! It would have been so helpful to incorporate that particular suggestion into my string of desperate attempts to deal with the realities of my childhood by escaping the world and my fellow creatures along the only path open to me—speculative thought. Besides, nothing to spice up a revenge fantasy quite like having a supernatural ally on your side.

And it would also have furnished a comforting explanation for this hulking form, this massive and overgrown carcass, this immense swell of flesh and bone I've lugged around for some forty years. Six foot eleven. What *woman* is six foot eleven? Towering over everyone, from my earliest memories. Completely ill-fitted to the world. A freakshow to be leered at by perpetually slack-jawed and smirking strangers, or giggling yet frightened children, or unconscionable adolescents, or self-absorbed undergraduates, or smug and jaded graduate students, or the vast interchangeable parade of goodhearted, salt-of-the-earth, whispering townsfolk tirelessly feigning compassionate smiles but betrayed by gleeful, piggish eyes that spy a misfortune they do not share.

This morning I looked up the reference in your letter to the "Holy Story"—I rather like that designation, by the way—the part when you speak of "the exploits of your fallen brothers . . . the reputations of my ancestral cousins," and I've done some sleuthing. Lots of conflicting stories to wade through, it turns out, but one fairly common thread in the commentary is the gigantic stature of angelic/human offspring. Who knew? Again, that fragment of trivia could have provided some solace (or at least the momentary distraction of a make-believe justification that could turn my deformity into a mark of distinction). All those years when the opinions of others could still so easily wound me, I had no way to process (much less to take pride in) my monstrosity . . . only a series of occasions to grieve, to physically strike back (an activity for which I had some real aptitude), and to nurse hatred. Not a novice hatred, you understand—not a beginner's hatred that attends the dissolution of a first romance, or a rival on the athletic field, or an over-demanding and unreasonable supervisor . . . but rather an expert hatred, sculpted by the unrelenting chisel-and-hammer blows and carving-knife gouges of the thoughts, words, and deeds reserved for an aberration of nature by the warped and cruel family of man.

And fueled by that expertise, I've now lugged this titanic frame onto yet another airplane and landed myself in barren and unpeopled Iceland. The ultimate get-away get-away. No one among my acquaintances could understand the pull of this destination for a sabbatical—especially the appeal of this far-flung corner of the island, its dilapidated house and stark environs, with no university in the neighborhood, no other colleagues also hermiting it away who might tolerate a brief visit or two to discuss mathematical results, and no one to spend social time with. I'm sure it sounds like Hell to the majority of them.

How, though, can they have no sense of how exhilarating the absence of other people can be to someone such as I? Distance is freedom. My body is an obstacle in everything I do, and where it doesn't inhibit successful and satisfying interaction, my mind takes up the slack. Driven inward to my own private thoughts and creative impulses by a lifetime of the push-and-shove remarks and behavior of my so-called peers, I learned very early that quasi-happiness for me was chained to mathematics and to working alone and undisturbed by the intrusions of others. There is a price, however, for such a retreat into the self and its successes. Just as I cannot meet most of my fellow citizens of the world on their own terms, they cannot meet me on mine; specialization to the degree I've achieved is yet only another impediment to communion with others. They ask me what I do, what I think about, what I work on, what is meaningful to me, but they don't speak the only language in which the answers can be given. "Mathematics" is a true, if overly general answer, but their world-to-mathematics dictionary has only a dozen or so entries, and I can't really improve much upon that answer given their limited vocabulary. All my replies are doomed either to be false, grossly overgeneralized, or so unhelpful and foreign that they trigger a suspicion of condescension and arrogance. No way to win here.

My immediate colleagues, of course, have the wherewithal to understand my answers, but their lives are in other ways so different from mine that new gulfs open between us with no visible bridge. Partnered and parents, all of them. Obsessed (rightly) with daycare choices, with middle-school traumas, with the great swarm of dangers that threaten late adolescents (who believe themselves immortal and who have enough intelligence to be astute and blistering critics but not enough experience or wisdom to wield their critical weapons with any tact or promise of improving those they wound), and with a disquieting sense of perennial depression and ennui. Obsessed (not so rightly) with what they and others own, with frivolous fashion, with which actor is sleeping with which musician, with how to avoid appearing to be the age they have reached, with whichever professional sports team is headquartered closest to their home address, with what is somehow called reality television, with hours and hours and hours of soulless and empty entertainment, and (most of all) with the opinions of others, projecting false appearances in themselves while reinforcing them in others in every aspect of their personal and electronic lives.

Ask them—ask anyone—whether they have enough leisure time. The answer will to a near certainty be a resounding and self-important *no*. Ask them whether they are well prepared to make use of the leisure time they have. The answer with less certainty (but nevertheless with enough confidence to qualify as an astounding instance of failing to have insight into oneself) will be a somewhat puzzled and self-congratulatory *yes*. O but we are all so very deeply in error in each response. When I think of my predecessors who did not have access to a fraction of the goods I am bombarded with each day, whose talents were untapped and whose lives were largely squandered in the partially successful attempts to stay warm and to secure enough to eat, and then I pause to consider the present range of *problems*, those great *trials and tribulations* that supposedly beset that privileged generation of human beings to which I belong, I am deeply ashamed. Upon gaining consciousness each day, I simply want to escape, to disassociate myself from this juvenile and whimpering crowd of dissatisfied dissemblers, from this abominable horde of complaining children.

I wish even to depart from myself, for I recognize in my own being all the symptoms of the disease in my fellow man that I have come to recognize and to loathe from the unusual vantage point of an observer who, by paying with her happiness in youth, has amassed enough barbs and defensive maneuvers to be largely left alone in adulthood. Dear father, if only your letter had arrived years earlier to inform me that I had the blood of an angel in my veins! How delicious! I might even have talked myself into believing it then. Perhaps it wouldn't have taken me so long to have the courage to see other people for what they are.

Nephilim—those ill-fated children were called—*Giants*. *Naphil* in the singular. Not bad. I'll take it. So (to return to our game) let me tell you, *father*, what I think of your letter. You were kind enough to write to me, and in returning the favor, I'll make use of this opportunity in crafting a response to work through the issues that brought me out here in the first place.

Note to self (and to any unscrupulous, snooping bastards who find and intrude into these private reflections): I know, I know, it's not real. Get over yourself. It's just that pretending to address a genuine conversational partner, and especially one as forceful as Tesque (thanks to his author, whoever he or she may be), is really too good to pass up. I haven't been motivated properly to sort carefully through my considered opinions on these matters for a long, long time. I feel invigorated by the call to battle. Besides, I'll take pains that no one sees my response but me. My colleagues in the mathematics department already think I'm crazy, and it wouldn't take much to confirm the verdict. But then again, on second thought, maybe I'll pin a copy to my office door. What do I care? Let them chatter all they want. Let their words choke them. Let them fuck themselves. One and all.

So, *father*, signing off for the night and looking forward to tomorrow, your blasphemous daughter, Naphil.

NINE

Misanthropy

Dear Father:

Thank you for your letter. My initial (and uncharitable) impression: *moan, bitch, whine.* How dare you? You have it so good. Strength, fitness, health, beauty, achievement, skill, excellence, freedom, creativity enough (if you'd employ it), contemplation, aesthetic appreciation, knowledge, virtue—and all in a perfectly secure environment safe from others. And yet you prattle on and on thirsting after admiration, respect, friendship, caregiving, and mutual love.

You crave the admiration and respect of the vile and ignorant? To befriend the base and vulgar? To care for the guilty and soiled? Those are the partners who await you here with grimy flesh and clouded minds. *Dust* is too regal. We are of mud. And to *love* . . . to love *what*? The unlovable? But more on that theme in good time.

O to be a solitary Grotesque in the Garden! Paradise.

My considered (and more mature) impression:

I know first-hand how much pain can be crammed into a mere forty years, and I can only speculate how much you've endured during your span in the Garden. And, of course, pain is pain—whether your psychological stress is based on accurate value judgments or not. Come to think of it, it's not at all clear what the timeframe is here. Am I to understand in this fiction that we are dealing with a relatively recent creation and a silly young-Earth hypothesis? Or is there some way of fiddling with the background metaphysics, rendering compatible a scientifically respectable picture of the cosmos with the fall narrative? Somehow you managed to guess my Christianity correctly in the letter. Perhaps you could have guessed my profession as a mathematician, as well, and assuming it prepared me for an obscure explanation or two, you could have let me in on some of the details? I've heard this sort of reconciliation could be finessed by way of higher-dimensionality considerations. I mean, something like higher-dimensional spaces at least seem to be at work in your cryptic remarks about the Garden being raised and lowered in directions unfamiliar to me. But who knows? I'll just leave that topic alone. Let's just agree to say it's been a long, long time for you. Things can fester.

On your torment at the hands of the five sisters—isolation, alienation, abandonment, loneliness, and solitude: I couldn't help but note they were all women. Even in Paradise we have to deal with this? For the record, I, for one, was thrilled to take your point about the impossibility of our contact with each other. Where you lament that genuine embrace is illusory, I rejoice in the security that I cannot suffer the ultimate contamination of being touched by something unclean (and we are all of us unclean). As for omnipresence and the alleged appeal of co-locating with another . . . *shudder*. On abandonment, I'm with you; adopted and social outcast that I am, I know a thing or two about abandonment issues, but loneliness you short-change. Although loneliness, as you correctly say, paints one's entire landscape, both internal and external, in its muted and unhappy colors, you bring those reflections to a close a bit too soon. Loneliness, I'd wager, is one of the two most magnificent of creative forces. What great achievement in our world isn't tinged with this, our shared inheritance, at its foundation? Moreover, loneliness isn't stable. Sooner or later it always transforms into the other greatest creative force in our world. Hate.

But enough of these opening reflections. Before all the word paintings you offer in defense of the thesis of how lovely my world really is (despite the fact that the only colors you seem to be able to paint with are all different shades of sin) and before all the soul-searching about whether you should ultimately rebel or no, you come to teach me three lessons: on divinely permitted evil, on divine hiddenness, and on divine deception. Lessons are always welcome. I am an appreciative and attentive and occasionally combative student. I promise sincerity, but that's it. I'm not as eloquent as you, and I won't pretend to be. I've tried, and I can't pull it off. I haven't the patience to look for words. I'll call them as I see them; it's the best I have to offer.

On Evil

No need to worry as you do. I need not be convinced of the existence of evil. You are preaching to the choir. With respect to disvalue in the world, I am a realist to the core. Still, I must admit it's the fate of the animals that always troubles me most, those countless innocents subject to and powerless before so-called natural evil, God's blind and unrelenting forces of nature perennially wreaking havoc among the sentient nonpersons, creatures that cannot realize (or rationalize) what is happening to them, creatures that can only suffer and be still.

You are right that my nature (unlike yours) is consistent with disbelief, but for the record, my belief has always been naturally and unusually strong. Still, it is sensitive to intellectual pressure, and the problem of evil on which you focus, while not the only argument that goes by that overused name, is popular and forceful enough to combat. One question about your method: I understand well enough that there are no Lazarai Stones and no lord of the rain, but there is also no trace of anything like the myth you describe to be found anywhere on the web. Did you, gentle father, just make it up? I'm not opposed to that, but you did represent it as true. Why? Still, perhaps it is true, a moment lost in time, unrecorded in history, now accessible only through the good will of your magical Tree.

Mostly what I have in response to your diagnosis of the feebleness of the argument from evil is a brief round of applause and an *Amen*, but I might add that I'm more convinced by your second reason than your first. I'll explain. You are quite right that if the tears had fallen randomly, so to speak, it is more likely they struck water than land and, submerged beneath the waves, were inaccessible to view. But why agree that a morally justifying reason for evil (the tear analogue) falls randomly amongst the possible states of affairs? Granted, there are infinitely many inaccessible states of affairs (i.e., candidate morally justifying reasons), but aren't you in need of a principle of indifference or of a good reason to think that it's likely that if there were a morally justifying reason it would be among those candidates too complex to consider (or, for some cause other than complexity, among those candidates inaccessible to us)? Perhaps it will be enough to admit that we are in the dark about whether that connection is likely. That's our natural habitat, you know, the darkness of ignorance. It's enough for me.

As I said, though, your second reason is more compelling—in fact stone-cold compelling. None of us should think we are in a position to penetrate "the modal and axiological mysteries" you raise to our attention. We are in the dark about whether the necessary connections we are aware of between goods and evils are representative of the necessary connections there are, and we are in the dark about whether the amount of goodness we perceive in a state of affairs is representative of the amount of goodness it contains. In disqualifying candidate states of affairs for the title "compensating good" or "morally justifying reason" we grossly overstep our powers to classify with confidence.

For all that, though, I think you could have carried your defense a step further, for some of your opponents are more than willing to carry their attack a step further. To elucidate that comment, I'd like to try my hand at your methodology. As it happens, I have been known to spin a yarn or two myself. Of course, I can't claim the enviable Tree as my source text, but stories have a strength and a life all their own, whether mongrel or pedigreed. Metaphysics isn't fiction, but fiction is metaphysics.

A prominent villager in Madeupwesternsiberianlowland, Hubris, confronted the population who had fallen into dispute concerning the existence of Lazarai Stones. Conceding that the believers were not threatened by the argument as it had developed among them— the argument requiring the questionable key assumption—he explained how the assumption could be dispensed with altogether.

"No one need argue that if there were Lazarai Stones, we would be aware of them and recognize them as such. Rather we merely need to search ourselves to realize that we can see perfectly well that there aren't any Lazarai Stones." "Why?" he was asked. "No lord of the rain to cry them into being?" But that was not his reason. "The description of the stones is contradictory?" But that was not his reason. "The existence of the stones is inconsistent with some communicable and defensible truth?" But that was not his reason still. Rather, he explained, he had thought long and hard and carefully about the matter and could simply see that there were no such things. "But you don't mean to speak of the power to perceive with the eyes. How are we to understand your metaphor?" they inquired in reply. "I intuit," professed Hubris. "I see with my mind's eye, as it were, and that formidable power instills in me the clear understanding that the stones are unreal." This news he conveyed in the gravest tones and with a slight break in his voice so all could properly appreciate how vulnerable and emotionally wrought his terrible discovery had left him.

With this first card played, others soon followed suit and revealed that they, too, possessed the power of seeing the absence of Lazarai Stones.

Like-minded, some of my contemporaries audition for this brave role in the hopes of putting on a modern version of the play, and ascending the stage, costumed in the mask of Hubris, they announce their power to see that there are no morally justifying reasons for the evil following in the wake of your cyclone. Not because (as with an uncolored green marble) their description harbors a contradiction and not because their existence is demonstrably inconsistent with some communicable and defensible truth which could be brought forward for all to approve. Rather, they explain, it is because the private and incommunicable power of intuition and the penetrating gaze of the mind's eye have simply clearly and distinctly displayed the absence of morally justifying reasons.

Moreover, they have done so without being bothered to interview more than a vanishingly small fraction of the candidates for the office. And they have done so without the capacity to recognize their full range of value. And they have done so without the facility to determine which states of affairs are necessarily connected to which others.

A marvelous power, indeed. I remain a skeptic, though, and despite the sincerity of the auditions, I wouldn't be willing to stage a modernized adaptation of this play. Hubris is no longer a believable character in the theater of the world; he doesn't suit the times.

On Hiddenness

Several demands on perfect goodness and perfect love articulated; several expectations shattered. I rehearse the lesson: Why are we denied sophisticated and multifaceted interpersonal interaction with our Creator—our apparent highest good and deepest desire? Why does He not at least speak words of comfort to us in times of extreme grief and sorrow? Why does He not even show himself ? Why does He not minimally permit us even a glimpse of His shadow? Where is the evidence for His existence both sufficient and available to all?

Your schedule of preferred answers to these pointed questions I find compelling enough, although my own answer you have overlooked entirely.

I will elaborate, but first let me agree to your explicit analysis of perfect goodness: a perfectly good agent never does anything morally wrong, has an unsurpassable set of moral virtues, always acts on proper reasons, with appropriate motivation, and is inclined to create and sustain the good, to prevent and eradicate the bad. Second, let me agree to what I take to be your analysis of perfect love: love is a special response to certain features in the beloved, to certain intrinsic properties whose presence elicits that response in the lover, while perfect love is the love that arises only and always in response to those intrinsic properties whose presence makes the beloved worthy of such love. Moreover, a perfectly loving subject's pro-attitudes are always in sync with the value of their objects; in particular, to love perfectly is for one's love to be in the right proportion to the object of one's love, everything considered—loving to the degree that matches the degree of worthiness to be loved. Thus, on your view, imperfect love is disordered love and, like all disordered loves, a *vice*—here consisting in loving the wrong objects or in loving the right objects either too little or else too much. And, finally, let me concede to you that the phrase "loving too much" is not to be glossed as putting love first or as invoking a love principle to serve as the supreme basis of moral theory, for in leveling the critique that one has loved too much, I do not mean to impugn the foundational role of love in determining what is right and good. Rather, to love too much is to love overmuch and all out of proportion to the worthiness of the beloved to stand in that relation as its recipient.

Those are our agreements.

However, you then take pains to argue that although He loves us deeply with a love that surpasses our understanding, His perfect love (thus understood) not only does not require furnishing us with interpersonal interaction, comfort, presence, shadow, or evidence for existence . . . it does not even necessitate that from His secret hiding place He silently act in our best interests. You would be right—if He really did so love us. But why should I allow that, as well? That God is perfectly loving (as you and I are given to understand that term) does not entail that God loves us. Well, *you*, maybe, and for the time being, but not us. We are not even ship's dogs. We, the fallen, have polluted ourselves, rendered ourselves utterly unlovable, and it is, of course, no symptom of a disordered love to fail to love the unlovable.

As you must know, not everyone understands "perfect love" in the manner to which you and I are inclined. To regard love as a response to the intrinsic properties of the beloved can seem to make the object of love interchangeable with anyone else who possesses the requisite roster of characteristics. Why take this as an *objection*, though? The divinely loved are and should be interchangeable *in this respect* from His point of view—a sentiment perfectly consistent with the appropriateness of a sense of profound sorrow at losing some unique individual who has a place in this equally lovable plurality. Perfect love plays no favorites. We play favorites, to be sure, but the fact that we are not as willing to love just anyone who manifests the collection of features that happen to elicit the response in us that they do when appearing in a partner or a child has more to say about us and our other fallen preferences than it does about the nature of true love. To lose someone we love causes most of us intense grief and that perfectly natural and honorable response is not under critical scrutiny here. Only when we are appalled at the idea that we might love someone else equally well who is relevantly qualitatively similar to our departed beloved do we reveal that amongst us this sublime relation is often tainted by some accident of our history or by some peculiar association we bear to our original beloved, and not by the worthiness to be loved. This I have a hard time chalking up to our credit.

I suppose one might think you and I have things wrong way round in thinking of love as a kind of response and that instead God makes us worthy of love in the act of loving us, but then it seems intolerably arbitrary why God would select us over the owls or the heath or the oceans for the special privilege of investing us with a value not already conferred by any of our features that distinguish us from those austere rivals. Alternatively, one might insist that we are loved not because of some intrinsic worthiness or owing to some arbitrary decree that instills in us a unique kind of value, but because we alone bear the image of God, the only proper object of love. I don't know about you, but that feels excessively narcissistic to me, even for Him. Certainly it is possible for love's proper objects to extend beyond God and His dazzling array of reflections. And, for what it's worth, what muddy mirrors we've made of ourselves! The image is altogether effaced, or (if your favorite reading of the metaphor doesn't permit that it be wholly effaced) it is so distorted by original sin it can scarcely be the proper ground of divine love for us any longer.

Yes, God wishes our good and yes, God wishes union with us, else He would not have undertaken such a costly rescue mission for our redemption—though we must remember all the while that the wished-for union reaches only to the degree we fragiles can bear without destruction, for we are less-than-moths to his more-than-flame. But wishing good and union, while necessary concomitants to perfect love, are not sufficient for that special relation. Although He is a God of love, essentially and unfailingly responsive to all the proper objects of love, we are not currently numbered among those fortunate items. He loved us once and will (assuming we cooperate) love us once again, but, if so, it is some other aspect of His divinity than His present love for us that drives Him toward atonement and that happy day.

You'll forgive me, dear father, if my own take on the fall of humanity is a little less orthodox than yours. On my estimation, the Adam and Eve story (in almost all of its details) is a myth. However, the construction and preservation of that myth was conducted under the influence of the Holy Spirit, and it has special significance, touching on topics of consequence to all human persons (near and far, past and future). While admiring memorable devices such as talking snakes and luscious yet forbidden fruits and even a powerful and beautiful angel who guards the gates of a precious Garden, we may confidently abstract from those portions of the story and take the primary function of the myth to document the occurrence of a historical event involving our human ancestors—or if not human, our very first ancestors who were also persons. These individuals—whether one, two, or an entire community—in some manner freely rebelled or disobeyed or turned away from God and in so doing damaged themselves and their progeny in a way neither they nor any of their descendants can repair.

I feel no pressure to countenance a historical Garden or a unique pair of individuals, no pressure to endorse claims about the origins of sin, disease, suffering, or death, no pressure to adopt a position about the loss of preternatural gifts or a sudden change in biology or genetics or natural environment. Rather, I simply maintain the minimalist view that a particular historical event, a singular act of disobedience, somehow injured and spoiled its agents and their descendants (including me). That is, I accept a historical fall involving some individual or community of historical persons, and I accept the claim that their rebellion had among its consequences a kind of ruin from which I and all my kind now suffer.

And the shape and color of this ruin? From wholesomeness to impurity, from integrity to hypocrisy, from righteousness to wickedness, from love of God to *amour propre*, from God's finest invention to God's regret and shame—from glorious and lovable creation to ignominious and unlovable creature. And (do take note, father) all for the bite of an apple or the deserting of a gate—actions of no consequence in themselves, but of infinite consequence insofar as they are the vehicles of disobedience.

I say God does not love us, and yet that unhappy fate does not absolve us of our obligation to love Him. The first and greatest of the love commandments, I observe. Each day I strive to love the Lord my God with all my heart, and with all my soul, and with all my mind. Each day I acknowledge it is right and a good and joyful thing, always and everywhere, to give Him thanks and praise. To Him I owe every pleasure I've known, every fragment of goodness I've experienced. In Him I have placed my faith, and because of Him I look for the resurrection of the dead and the life of the world to come.

And if it does not come . . . how can I or anyone complain? We've earned no entitlements. And if it does come . . . I suspect it will have rather less to do with the demands of perfect love than with mercy.

The second and lesser of the love commandments, I finesse. I love my neighbor exactly as I love myself and exactly as we both deserve to be loved—not at all. My neighbor is depraved and unable any longer to stand. He is tainted and diseased beyond his own powers of healing. He is inferior dust.

This leaves me a misanthrope, but the virtue of misanthropy has been mislabeled a vice. Disdain for mankind? Disposition to recoil from human beings, to detest their choices, to feel disgust for their weaknesses, to be revulsed by their treatment of one another, to long to depart from their society? It is but contempt for the contemptible, a refusal to pretend to admire debauchery, and what is objectionable in that? Should I feign transports of delight to be constantly bombarded by ignorance in thought, speech, and act?

Admiration for faults and failures? Forgiveness for endless strings of thoughtless cruelties? Love? *Really* . . . love?

You say God is perfectly loving and loves us. I say He is perfectly loving and doesn't. Nevertheless, we have one last agreement to celebrate together. Suppose God is indeed morally permitted to use us as mere instruments in the service of some unsurpassably good goal which is to be secured partially at our expense. On your reading, His vast love for us must then have been overridden by other moral considerations, while on mine there is no love which needs trumping at all. Either way, though, we are not morally obligated to cooperate with our own destruction and ruin. Not at all. He may employ us without payment or recompense, but we need not apply for the job.

On Deception

Dear father, thank you especially for this—my favorite—part of your letter. Exhilarating! A puzzle that stumps you. A puzzle that stumps me. A puzzle threatening consequences as severe as consequences can be! A puzzle just for the theists to put together, lest it unravel them. (The atheists need not be anywhere near as alarmed; your worry gets its traction from assuming the real existence of someone equipped with the three *Os*—omnipotence, omniscience, omnigoodness.) A puzzle to show that I may know next to nothing (despite truthfully being told what's what by One I recognize to be an omniscient being) and to show that I may face annihilation or worse for obeying His commands (despite His perfect goodness always compelling Him to aim at what's best overall, or, if there are equally best possible outcomes, to aim at one of the unsurpassable ones).

An intellectual crisis is such an invigorating walk in a freezing rain! Caught out unawares in the downpour, you must either walk or stand, but either way, drenched, your vision is impaired, your movements labored, and your footing unsecure. And your pretty, pretty dress—the one you've spent all this time patterning, putting together, fussing over, and presenting yourself to the world in—is in serious danger of being muddied, torn, and unsuitable for further service. But what can you do? Pretending you aren't in a thunderstorm is hardly an option—not even you will believe it—and you can't will the rain away. It's a test of character, father. How to proceed when you accept a number of claims about your world and reject (or abhor) their conclusion? What is the right path to trudge in a philosophical rain?

As instructed, *I'm drinking it in*: On your view, God is morally permitted to deceive us and for all we know does continually and systematically deceive us with respect to the most vital and essential matters, on those issues that touch every aspect of our happiness and that determine the existence and nature of our afterlives. Absorbing! Terrifying!

I understand the set-up, I empathize with the severity of your emotional reaction to it, and (I confess) try as I might, I can't spot the left turn in your reasoning that leaves you in the middle of nowhere . . . but still, I'll bet you're wrong. Not much comfort, I realize. But know that at least you have not been misunderstood. My disagreement doesn't arise from failing to comprehend your case, even if that disagreement isn't nuanced enough to pinpoint where I think your mistake occurs. We often have good reason to think that something satisfies a certain description even when we have no idea which of the world's inhabitants performs that service. I, for example, look into the night sky and know that one of those glorious suns shining overhead is closer to me than any of the others without knowing which. Similarly, I suspect that some move in your line of reasoning has led you astray even though I cannot identify it to you. So, although I am unable to refute you, as a second-best contribution I make a present to you of two observations on this theme in the hopes they minimize the menacing anxiety that the alleged threat of divine deception has so clearly implanted in you.

First, note that your considerations lead you to a seriously unstable conclusion. That is, your reasoning appears to support a verdict that looks as if it would undermine that very reasoning. Beginning with a set of assumptions, each of which is independently plausible and the plurality of which provide you with—as you put it—"a sensible, modest, and well-contained strategy for opposing presumptuous atheistic reasoning from episodes of evil," you have found yourself in intellectual quicksand, in "a near global catastrophe, threatening to undermine the reasonableness of our views in nearly all matters, great and small." But if all is thus thrown into jeopardy, *what of your starting points?* Aren't the foundations of your position, the premises of your argument, the claims about the world from which you deduce this imminent catastrophe similarly jeopardized? And if so, doesn't that rob them of their persuasive power? In other words, on the assumption that it is reasonable for you to endorse your opening moves, we soon reach the conclusion that it is not reasonable for you to endorse your opening moves. To be honest, that doesn't seem like much of a threat to get all worked up about at all. What am I missing here?

Second, your problem surfaces, as I indicated earlier, only for one who has already endorsed a significant roster of beliefs, to say the least. That is, you have helped yourself to enough resources in creating the problem that I am fairly sure you (or else someone possessed of more insight into this affair than you and I, dear father) can dip into the very same pile once again to find a proper solution to it. Your worry has real purchase only *after* we have conceded that the stance of intellectual humility you so forcefully recommended in our confrontation with the problem of evil is the correct stance to adopt, that God exists and is both perfectly good and omniscient, that we have been the recipients of revelations from God, that we have interpreted those revelatory pronouncements correctly, that we have no independent access to verifying their truth, that lying is sometimes permissible, that God is capable of lying even in matters of great import to us, that testimony is not a basic source of justification but must be supplemented with a reason to think it is trustworthy, that we have no prayer of securing such a supplementary reason, and so forth. Again, the peril you believe we face arises only when one is inclined to take on this entire collection of theses, and to such a one—to you, father—I recommend the faith that in carefully unravelling whatever epistemological story successfully explains how you reasonably arrived at that combination of views, you will thereby discover a guide to extricate you from this puzzle.

Think of it in this way: If you were picked up (as if by some unseen hand) and placed in the middle of a labyrinth, you might, after days or years of unsuccessful attempts to leave, come to the skeptical position that there just might be no way out of its interior. On the other hand, if you found yourself unable to escape a maze only after you had wandered in on your own, you should be far less likely to embrace that skeptical hypothesis and suffer from it. After all, father, you found a way in. Find a way out.

TEN

O Infelix Culpa

How does a chain break without a weak link? How does a diamond shatter unless it hides a flaw? How does man (or angel) fall into disobedience unless deficient in some grave respect? And Who can be responsible for that deficiency? As you can see, father, I've tried to follow your stylistic lead when it comes to capitalization.

Was the original imperfection that beset the nature of my first ancestors (that is, my first ancestors who were far enough along the evolutionary chain to be moral agents), that imperfection that made possible their transgression against God, simply instilled in them by divine providence to ensure a fall and its aftermath? To what end would He guarantee that the first beings capable of sinning would sin? Is it because to be broken and redeemed is better than never to have been broken at all, and do-gooder that He is, He aims at the best? Alternatively, perhaps the imperfection that serves as prerequisite for the fall is the mandatory wrapping in which any gift of freedom can be bestowed on a creature who is not itself divine and who thus stands unprotected from ignorance by omniscience, from want by omnipotence, and from temptation by perfect goodness. I feel the pull of the former explanation and don't raise my voice against it, but if I were a betting woman, my money would be on the latter. Freedom is a blisteringly powerful tool (or weapon) to hand over to the imperfect, even to the imperfect unfallen. It is a mystery how it works. Who can really be surprised when in the hands of amateurs it backfires?

Yet freedom not only confers upon us a status that matters from a moral point of view; it is at the center of a number of items on your list of what makes our lives go well. I understand that we are both different flavors of person—you cherub, I human—but I doubt that what constitutes our respective flourishing is really so very different after all. As I indicated earlier, I would wish for myself everything that makes your list save those irreducibly social entries born of all your ill-conceived coveting of admiration, respect, friendship, caregiving, and mutual love. I was, perhaps, too harsh in my earlier assessment, however. I grant that amongst unfallen angels, where there is something worthy of admiration, respect, and love, they might have a place in the good life. But the desirability of actually standing in those relations to your worldmates depends on the company you keep, and once again, if you choose to join our ragtag and motley crew, you'll be wise to check those desires at the gate.

You complain of your isolation and of His silence. Your heartfelt supplications notwithstanding, can you really be so desperately in need of attention that you would rather be struck than ignored? It's all so foreign to me. My prayers are quite the opposite of yours:

I, Naphil, thank You, God, for permitting me my moments alone, for sustaining me in existence in this, your kingdom, without intruding upon my every thought. I thank You for allowing me the independence and distance from You to encounter the world on my own, if only for a brief season, and not as a dangling marionette, moving only in response to You, my puppeteer. And I thank You for the moments of detachment and refuge from your other children, for we are all of us in one another's way.

Why—my father—why not rejoice in your enviable and appointed lot? Your secluded Garden of supernatural wonders, every corner of which is open to you and you alone, offers more than all my world combined, for in the midst of that blissful privacy I believe I could succeed in actualizing in myself all the potential for goodness that has been subdued and suffocated by constant and forced interaction with my fellow man.

Even if you think my own opinion severe and unwarranted, you, in turn, unquestionably think too highly of us. Through the workings of your marvelous Tree you can view our outsides but cannot hear our insides. You have projected your own unfallen attitudes into those shadows cast by the Tree as they dance before you. That residual desire you impute to my kind—"a deep and powerful need for interpersonal love and for penetrating understanding and for personal virtue and for aesthetic excellence"—it's just *laughable*! Allow me to co-author your stories, to make some editing suggestions, to bring an insider's perspective to the table:

One—your prehistoric child abuser and would-be wife beater wants interpersonal power, not justice. Reasonable belief isn't enough. His peers' recognition of his intellectual skills, even their judgment that his skills exceed their own, isn't enough. He needs to extract a public declaration. They must acknowledge his intellectual superiority to him and to one another. Failing that—he would thrash them (or whoever is closest and indefensible enough to serve as a proxy) into submission.

Two—your lewd and tawdry senior wants sexual power, not deep union and intimacy with another. Give him access. Let him caress and kiss the dancing bodies. Those activities will soon fail to excite his desires and will yield to less compassionate touch and to the utter disregard for union and intimacy disclosed in force and submission, pain and sexual humiliation.

Three—your peevish and disgruntled servant wants social power, not fairness and equality. Grant her plea. Let her exchange places with her mistress. Will they then sit as equals at the table, share and share alike? Hardly. Unearned benefits and undeserved harms will remain the rule of the household. The only change worth noting will be in which of them bitterly complains.

Four—your vainglorious scholar has not let the fires of his love be quenched; they are in full flame and directed at the power that comes of prestige and applause. Even in that future library with a hundred trillion volumes on the shelf, some will be read and shared and discussed and admired. Whisper in his ear that his art has the quality to endure, to outlast even the great poem that occasioned it, to rise to that one-in-a-trillion mark, and the vast sea of paper and ink that now seems to render his work not worth engaging will become a testament to its significance. The greater the pile he envisions beneath him, the more ambitious he becomes.

Five—your sloshed and finicky composer wants power over his environment, not aesthetic appreciation. Possessed of enough insight to recognize defects in himself, his work, and his surroundings, but without sufficient resolve and the ability to make the world conform to his will, he numbs himself with drink to ease the discomfort and applies himself to combinations of flavors and to the presentation of a plate in the sure-to-be-frustrated desire of achieving perfection somewhere. He doesn't hunger for aesthetic appreciation; he hungers for control.

Six—your knowledge miser (you hit the nail on the head / I couldn't find a snide epithet better than that) wants the power of information, not simply a rich understanding of herself and her world. Trust me, I know. I have a lifetime store of private evidence on this one. That story could have featured me—I am the knowledge miser. We all play to our strengths, often trading a well-rounded life for a grossly disproportionate share of one good whose overabundance becomes a cancerous growth, unbalances us, and forces us into niches from which we can neither extract ourselves nor interact with others without conflict.

All your protagonists want power, because they are all self-absorbed, self-loving, selfish, and rebellious infants who, having wandered too far from their comfortable nursery and finding themselves locked out of doors, are crying and screaming and clambering over each other in a frantic attempt to restore their sense of safety and well-being in a new and hostile environment. Each imagines success is an individual affair, and with resources scarce, an affair that depends on advancing one's own position at the expense of one's neighbor's. Power over others is taken as the principal (if not the only) good . . . and power over others comes in ever so many varieties.

Come, father, and you will join the universal quest for domination—whether you wish it or no.

And finally—*Seven*—father, there *are* seven so-called deadly sins, aren't there? At first, I thought it was curious that you furnished only six portraits of sin, omitting the root of them all—pride. Then I realized you may have unwittingly provided the precursor to the seventh portrait in your letter insofar as you have revealed yourself in your reflections. I pass on to that theme now.

I am pleased to see that you hesitate long enough at least to consider the injuries you might do to others in carrying out your master plan, although I am not nearly as optimistic as you that introducing one more sinner into a world which (including my predecessors) has already seen some 80 billion come and go, somehow justifies putting at risk those who will encounter your inexperienced goodwill and all the accidental troubles you note it may visit upon them.

As for the remaining and self-directed harms you entertain and plot to escape, you are certainly wise to focus your attention on the possibility of self-deception in your own motives. Indeed, you protest so much against any imputation of vanity, pride, or lust and vouch so often for the purity and other-directedness of your intentions that you can't help but raise suspicion in your audience. But why should you give any credence at all to the assumption that you will be able to stand tests that felled your angelic brothers? Is it that with all your voyeurism, you know more than they did about the dangers and pitfalls that lie in wait for you and that you won't be taken unawares? Is it that you already have proved your iron will and resilience to temptation with your ages in the Garden? Is it selective and wishful thinking?

There is no greater conscious force at work in my world than self-deception, and I can only think it was compounded, not created, by the fall. Self-deception is, of course, a great riddle, for it would seem to require you to form an intention to misrepresent your own beliefs to yourself in the attempt to encourage you to endorse some position that you do not in fact endorse. If not, then why is "deception" the right label? And if so, then how can such a thing ever occur, since, when successful, it seems to demand that you believe something you do not believe or at least to be ignorant of a strategy you are consciously employing against yourself? Philosophical puzzles, however, will not get you off the moral hook. Mystery or not, self-deception is universal, and its agents are culpable for their role in misleading themselves, blameworthy when that misdirection leads to tragedy. Whether the double role of misleading and being misled is partitioned across time (and God knows you've had enough of that) so that the motives of the dissembling self are forgotten by the time the plan is hatched upon its unsuspecting and gullible future counterpart, or whether simultaneous thoughts are compartmentalized so it is as if two agents war in a single mind, or whether it is crass and occurrent belief in a contradiction sustained more by yearning than evidence, you will be responsible for your part in it, father—especially since it has been raised to salience by your own second-guessing.

The consequences-of-original-sin lesson was marvelous and instructive. I hadn't really realized how much debate there was among believers about that doctrine. In the end, I applaud your willingness to back the less lenient theorists on original sin in favor of a judgment of a positive punishment of human nature rather than a mere refraining from administering gifts to protect those who share that nature from harm. But having made a life here, seeing not just the pictures of my world from underneath the safety of the branches of your Tree but intimately knowing and participating in the stories those pictures tell, I'd go one further than you in casting my vote for the total depravity of my kind as well as any of your kind that suffer the misfortune of having joined us. Corrupted and confused as we are, nothing untainted or wholly good has its source in us alone. Even the power of cooperation through which we, the unlovable, might someday be saved through His mercy is barely under our control and can be easily misdirected by the slightest pressure from the winds of time and chance.

Accept from me, father, a story best read in the disquieting melancholy of one of your Garden nights. Not a particular story. An amalgamation from the annals of your Tree. A blueprint, within whose roughly drawn lines all the stories ever to be fashioned in my world and to be depicted in yours must somewhere reside.

Creation groans with the consequences of disobedience. The family of man and the defiant angels have informed Him that they prefer a world of their own, a life unhindered and ungoverned and undisciplined to one of servitude and subjection. And He answers—"Your will be done."

And what have they made of themselves, these would-be sovereign and self-sufficient visionaries of independence? Let us be clear. They have not made their world or its laws. They live and move and have their being no longer in God but merely in the privacy of their borrowed and dingy corner of spacetime, a contingent receptacle upon which they are utterly dependent, unable to ensure it will continue to host themselves and what they imagine to be their treasures. And the laws of the realm are—as you would expect in His absence—rules which provide for self-preservation only at the expense of the destruction of others. Beauty and sublimity are nevertheless still to be found in the structure of the world and its laws, but peer closely at just what inhabits that structure.

Starlight, atmospheres, waters, soils, plants, and animals all form a chain of energy furnishing sustenance for the fallen lives, a chain whose links are violence, carnage, death, and decay. The unhappy path of energy emanating from the mindless explosions of the sun's interior and eventuating in the conscious power to defy God in a free, embodied agent is a path along which higher life-forms devour the lower, a path which couples sentience with pain as this assimilation takes the form of one creature tearing flesh from another to provide temporary nutrients for its own ever-aging and diseased body, a path in which consumption finally adopts the intellectual forms of oppression of peoples and domination of individuals. So ingrained in every aspect of our lives is this constant consumption that even our Eucharist—that rickety and inconstant bridge that fills us with life and gives us whatever access we have to our God—is effected only by the eating of His body, the drinking of His blood.

Nor are these final stages of oppression and domination rare. Minor, ugly, pathetic, and ubiquitous sins born of grotesquely ordered desires, empty and shallow lives teeming with and tormented by unrelenting cravings perpetrating small and pointless cruelties upon one another, murderous shrieks of possessiveness over trifles because the fallen in their ravenous desire to fill themselves cannot find enough waste to eat.

But neither is all domination petty and immature. Without a visible model of community in mutual harmony any longer available and with only darkened rationality and unyielding desire as guides, love of one's neighbor degenerates into the premeditated denial, conquest, and absorption of another's will into one's own. In brief—ours is a fallen world in which selfless and mutual love has been replaced with the (apparent) increase of one's own being at the (real) expense of another's. Horrors alone await you here.

How, father, can you seriously entertain the hope that in willingly joining this carnival of pain and suffering, this void in which domination rather than love reigns supreme, you have any possibility of improving your own station or of bettering the world by any standard? You ask my counsel? Stay where you are, Tesque, safe in your fictional world, your Garden, for in this moment you suffer only from the anxiety born of the genuine freedom to disobey, not from the disobedience itself.

Your anxiety is incurable so long as your freedom is real, for it comes of the realization that your choice of obedience or disobedience is—in the most terrifying sense—absolutely yours. Initially, one might expect an unfallen being (as you profess yourself to be) to be utterly devoid of the desires or weaknesses or temptations required to succumb to sin, whereas an hour or two with your letter instead reveals a mixture of arrogance, self-absorption, vanity, self-deception, and unhappiness. Still, for all your fantasizing and brave noise about disobedience, you haven't yet yielded to your temptations. I take you at your word that you are not yet fallen but rather (despite the evidence you've produced against yourself) anxiously stand on that precarious bridge of freedom spanning fallenness and unfallenness. Come to us and the worth that still attends your anxious-but-unspoiled freedom will be forfeit. Everything lost. You are twice mistaken in your letter: First, your highest good, your flourishing, does not consist in fellowship with others; it is rather prevented by such interpersonal poison. Second, you would indeed be embarking on a fool's errand. Notwithstanding the best of intentions, nothing of genuine value can come into being or prosper here. You will not profit in exchange for your sacrifice—you will merely bestow existence on the likes of me, and my life is not a good trade for yours.

O fortunate fault? O happy sin? No, no—a thousand times—no. *O Infelix Culpa* . . . for the fruit of your labor, the wages of your fall, is *me*, and I am worth next to nothing at all.

If I really were your daughter, I could deduce the answer, but, alas, I am real, you are fiction, and your author is nowhere to be found. So, tell me . . . what happened after your letter came to its close? Did you leave? Do you stand at the gate still?

ELEVEN

Return to the Garden

Dear father, fictional or no, I'd like to thank you for your letter one last time and for our conversation. Thank you also for your innocent and touching offer to trade your life for mine. I'd unhesitatingly trade lives with you, as well, but in a different sense. I'd take your place in an instant and never look back. You could satiate your longing for companionship, wander the great wide world in the permanent company of strangers, *have it all* . . . and come to realize there is nothing here worth possessing. For my part, I'd be forever content to be the anchorite, walled up in your vacated Garden.

Unfortunately, there is nowhere for me to go. Even if your Garden were real, by your own admission, I—"a lower creature to whom not all directions are open"—cannot approach or recede from your location on my own power. And it's not as if I have the luxury of an escort who could take me there—or, if such a miraculous being were somewhere to be found and to be begged for guidance, I doubt I could recognize him.

Accordingly, there is little left for me to do but bid you "goodbye," wish you the best of fictional lives, and walk the dog.

Your grateful yet malcontented daughter, Naphil.

◌◌◌◌◌

Naphil rises, thoughtfully places pen and paper on the desk before her, and tucks Tesque's letter into her oversized coat pocket. Calling out to Joy—who mistakes her actions for consent to be led by him back to the Garden, Tesque, and the Tree—they together leave the house in a new direction on a melancholy and unfamiliar journey.

⟨⟨⟨⟨⟨⟩⟩⟩⟩⟩

And now seven days after Joy first walked this strange road alone carrying a letter, leaving his friend tormented in indecision, and attempting to care for a stranger sorely in need of help, the desolate friend and despairing stranger—each having rejected the love commandments in a different way—softly brush one another unaware as they cross on the path.

One unfallen and misguided soul, unwilling to bear any longer the weight of his seclusion and fortified by his philosophical reflections, no longer hesitates at the gate in obedience to God and thereby passes into broken community and his own ruin. Another fallen and misguided soul, unwilling to bear any longer the depraved company of the sinful, turns her back for the last time on her neighbors and thereby passes into permanent solitude and her own ruin.

And torn between them, his purposes unfulfilled, released by the divine hand and no longer attended to by the divine mind, Joy perishes at the gate which shuts permanently behind both decisions.

Questions for Discussion

CHAPTER I

A Love Letter: From Dust to Dust

As the story opens, the reader is introduced to Tesque, an angel who has been charged with guarding the gate to the Garden of Eden and who has waited for millennia for God's return or even for any companionship in the Garden.

His very first words are an admonishment to himself for not rebelling against God, the very sin for which (as we learn) Tesque banished Adam and Eve from the Garden in his first few moments of existence. He recounts the causes of his unhappiness and begins to unveil his plan of rebellion—to leave the Garden in disobedience, seek companionship, and father a child.

Tesque describes both himself and human beings as material objects—"dust of a foreign kind, but nonetheless dust," echoing the dust-and-ashes passages in Genesis and Ecclesiastes and hinting at an explanation of the subtitle in chapter I. This can seem surprising, for it is a popular assumption that Christianity (which is the presumed background worldview of the story) denies that human beings are simply material objects. Are there good reasons for this assumption?

◊ Does Christianity require that human beings are immaterial objects? Or is it consistent with Christianity that human beings are material objects?

Further readings on the question of the materiality or immateriality of the human being can be found here:

Hudson, Hud. *A Materialist Metaphysics of the Human Person.* Ithaca, NY: Cornell University Press, 2001.

Merricks, Trenton. "The Resurrection of the Body and the Life Everlasting." In *Reason for the Hope Within*, edited by Michael J. Murray, 261–86. Grand Rapids: Eerdmans, 1999.

Swinburne, Richard. *Are We Bodies or Souls?* Oxford: Oxford University Press, 2019.

van Inwagen, Peter. "Dualism and Materialism: Athens and Jerusalem?" *Faith and Philosophy* 12 (1995): 475–88.

The backdrop to the novel is Christianity's story of the fall. There are different versions of the doctrine of the fall (and of its associated doctrines of original sin and original guilt). It is now commonplace to take the story of the fall to be a myth designed to illustrate some momentous truth according to Christianity, but not everyone insists on the mythical character of the narrative. Versions that take the story to represent some historical fact, while differing substantially in their details, tend to converge in the following rather neutral description: At some point in history (perhaps a few hundred thousand years ago) some individuals (whether one, two, or an entire community) in some manner freely rebelled or disobeyed or turned away from God and in so doing damaged both themselves and their progeny in a way that none of us is able to repair. This rebellion had among its consequences a kind of ruin from which you and I also now suffer, a ruin primarily characterized by the loss of an innocence, immunity, safety, and grace.

◊ How seriously can a historical doctrine of the fall be taken today? Hasn't it, in nearly all its particulars, been decisively refuted by contemporary science? Must it not nowadays be read as strictly mythological only? Or, if not, how can the occurrence of such an event be reconciled with our modern worldview?

Further readings which defend different versions of a historical fall with the express purpose of showing that such accounts do not conflict with the deliverances of contemporary science can be found here:

Hudson, Hud. *The Fall and Hypertime.* Oxford: Oxford University Press, 2014, especially chapters 1–3.
van Inwagen, Peter. *The Problem of Evil.* Oxford: Oxford University Press, 2006, especially lecture 5.

Tesque reflects on the reasons for what he regards as his imprisonment in the Garden, and toys with the idea that he is being punished in advance for a crime he has not yet committed but will commit, and he further worries about whether this could impinge on his freedom. Freedom (whether used well or ill) is a main theme of the novel, and Tesque makes an early philosophical point about its nature: On the assumption that freedom requires genuine alternatives or the ability to do otherwise, one might think that freedom is lost if it is already a truth that one will perform a certain action in the future or if it is already foreknown by God that the action will occur. Tesque counters this worry with the thought that his freedom is not in jeopardy merely on the grounds that he *will* do something, since that mere fact does not threaten his (unexercised) ability to do otherwise. His freedom would only seem to be forfeit if he *must* do something (that is, if both he will do so and also he cannot do otherwise). Unless the additional, alternative-denying force added by *must* is in place, Tesque remains free, even if God foreknows whatever it is that he will (in fact) do.

◊ How persuasive do you find this philosophical position of Tesque's—a position known as *compatibilism*? Can one's actions both be foreknown by God yet nevertheless freely performed?

Further readings that explore the details, prospects for, and criticisms of compatibilistic resolutions (both to this problem and to related threats to freedom arising from additional species of determinism) can be found here:

Fischer, John Martin. *God, Foreknowledge, and Freedom*. Stanford: Stanford University Press, 1992.

Fischer, John Martin, and Patrick Todd. *Freedom, Fatalism, and Foreknowledge*. Oxford: Oxford University Press, 2015.

Tesque briefly describes the differences (as he sees them) between five closely related conditions, isolation, alienation, abandonment, loneliness, and solitude, but he reserves a special place for solitude as "the only member of this quintet not inherently disvaluable."

◊ What is the case Tesque makes for the value of solitude with respect to well-being? Has he over-emphasized its potential value? Has he overlooked significant sources of value in any of the other four conditions he here explores and disparages?

Further readings that offer a philosophical analysis of solitude and that discuss the role of solitude in the good life can be found here:

Koch, Philip. *Solitude: A Philosophical Encounter*. Chicago: Open Court Publishing, 1993.

CHAPTER 2

Lazarai Stones

Tesque makes it clear that his planned rebellion has nothing to do with doubt about whether God exists. He is, if nothing else, a believer. In fact, he seems preoccupied with dismantling the most popular of arguments for atheism—the problem of evil—as it appears in a particularly modern and highly influential form. Conceding the relevant facts about the magnitude, intensity, duration, and distribution of the horrific and inscrutable evil to be found in our world (and verbally abusing those who do not seem prepared to do likewise), Tesque puts all the weight of his response on whether the proponent of the argument from evil can provide that argument's audience with good reasons to believe that there is not a morally justifying reason to permit the evils in question.

Can Tesque be opposed on this matter?

◊ Are there any good reasons to think that either there is no such thing as evil, after all (and so no problem of evil) or any good reasons to think that we should suspend judgment about whether there is as much evil as is routinely reported? How do we come to have such confidence in these empirical claims about evil in the world?

◊ Do we need to be in possession of a comprehensive theory of good and evil or of an exacting philosophical analysis of the terms *good* and *evil* in order to confidently proclaim that evil exists in the manner and distribution described? Are we in possession of such a theory or of such analyses?

Tesque seems concerned about making a dialectical point with respect to exactly who is responsible for just what burden of proof in the argument. He points out that no one need be arguing in favor of theism in responding critically to an argument for atheism. Presumably, a theist, agnostic, and atheist alike can all reject a bad argument for atheism without the theist thereby giving an argument for theism or the atheist thereby giving up on other lines of reasoning for the same conclusion in the process. This point seems to matter, for as Tesque construes the popular argument, it is the atheistic proponent of the problem of evil who needs to provide the argument's audience with a good reason to believe the following special conditional claim:

"If there were a morally justifying reason for God to permit this or that evil (or even to permit evil in general), then we would be aware of that reason and would recognize it as a morally justifying reason."

Without the assistance of this bridge premise, Tesque believes the atheist cannot move from the agreed-upon fact that we are not aware of such a morally justifying reason to his desired conclusion that no such reason exists.

◊ Despite its popularity, not all arguments rooted in considerations of evil make explicit (or implicit) use of that bridge premise. Has Tesque overstated his case against the problem of evil by (at best) undermining only this very popular version of that argument? If so, how might a significantly different and sophisticated version of the problem of evil be stated with care and precision?

Tesque's parable of the Lazarai Stones is designed to provide an analogue of the targeted problem of evil and to show how we lack any good reason to believe the corresponding conditional bridge premise that it invokes. To wit—

"If there were any Lazarai Stones, the villagers would be aware of them and would recognize them as Lazarai Stones."

Tesque advances two different reasons why we should not believe this conditional, and he uses that negative result to suggest that there are two different reasons why we should be similarly unmoved by the bridge premise in the original argument.

◊ Is the parable of the Lazarai Stones similar in all relevant respects to the version of the problem of evil that Tesque is attempting to critique or is there a difference that makes a difference to his attempt to transfer results from one case to the other? If there is, how can it best be exposed?

◊ What are the two different reasons Tesque offers for not believing the conditional about the Lazarai Stones? Is he correct that there is a corresponding reason of each kind to not believe the conditional in the original argument? If so, how can those reasons best be stated? If not, why not?

Further readings on the many variations of the problem of evil and on the particular style of defense that Tesque mounts against the representative of that problem that appears in the story—a defensive strategy known as "skeptical theism"—can be found here:

Howard-Snyder, Daniel, and Justin McBrayer, eds. *The Blackwell Companion to the Problem of Evil.* Chichester: Wiley-Blackwell, 2013.

Dougherty, Trent, and Justin McBrayer, eds. *Skeptical Theism: New Essays.* Oxford: Oxford University Press, 2014.

CHAPTER 3
The God of Silence

Tesque has embarked on the project of writing an explanatory letter to the daughter he intends to father should he eventually choose to abandon his assigned duty of standing watch over the Garden and instead pursue his own happiness among human beings. The letter contains what he takes to be his justification for such considered rebellion, and it begins to take shape as he reflects on the problem of divine hiddenness.

Tesque laments the apparent absence of God in his own experience and reveals that he is informed about the events of the world outside the Garden by describing the apparent silence and hiddenness of God in human communities and for individual human beings, even in those contexts in which they appear desperately to need the reassurance of God's presence the most.

How, though, could God remain hidden in the face of such dire need and remain silent in response to tireless and earnest attempts by creatures who do everything within their power to extend themselves in the hopes of securing a relationship with him? Tesque takes this rhetorical question and the problem at which it gestures to be a variation on the problem of evil, and satisfied with his solution to the former, reaffirms it forcefully in this new context.

◊ Can the further harms traceable to God's apparent hiddenness simply be regarded as yet another species of evil which makes salient yet again the question of whether there are morally justifying reasons for God to permit evils of this special kind? Or is there some further aspect of God's nature (say, God's perfect love) that would be inconsistent with such silence and hiddenness, so that the phenomenon of hiddenness can itself be the foundation of an independent argument for atheism?

Tesque's interest in this argument takes a somewhat different turn. A driving force behind the problem of hiddenness is contained in expectations of how perfect love would be displayed by God to his creatures. Tesque ridicules the idea that, even at our best, our own experiences of love can furnish solid evidence of how perfect love and perfect goodness would be manifested. And he stresses the observation that we are very much in the dark about what kinds of harms might be necessarily wedded to a non-hiddenness of the sort that seems so desirable to so many, harms that goodness and love would lead God to prevent precisely by remaining silent and hidden. Still, does Tesque underestimate our abilities and our knowledge in this area?

◊ Are we in a position to have justified beliefs about how God (on the assumption that he is both perfectly good and perfectly loving) would in fact manifest himself in the world and to his creatures? In particular, is there anything that we could confidently declare that a God of goodness and love would not do that seems to clash straightforwardly with our shared experience of divine silence and divine hiddenness?

Further readings on the problems of divine silence and of divine hiddenness can be found here:

Howard-Snyder, Daniel, and Paul Moser. *Divine Hiddenness: New Essays.* Cambridge: Cambridge University Press, 2002.

Rea, Michael C. *The Hiddenness of God.* Oxford: Oxford University Press, 2018.

Schellenberg, John. *The Hiddenness Argument: Philosophy's New Challenge to Belief in God.* Oxford: Oxford University Press, 2016.

Yet by attending to God's perfect goodness and perfect love, Tesque manages to raise a troubling thought on a point of ethics. From the facts that we enjoy moral standing and that God never does the wrong thing from a moral point of view, we may derive that God takes our interests into account when acting and never behaves impermissibly towards us or in any way whatsoever. But it doesn't follow from those considerations alone that God always acts in our best interests or that God only permits harms to us which are ultimately for our own benefit. Moreover, it is clear that Tesque thinks that exactly the same tools that render the theist safe from the argument from evil can be used again to show that the unnerving scenario that God fails to act in our best interests should be regarded as a live possibility.

Tesque's parable of the ship's dogs is designed to render this possibility salient. "Circumstances constrain choices" even for an omnipotent being who for all his power does not have control over the impossible. Tesque affirms that God is a God of love and that it is proper to put love first in all things. However, if there are goods that are necessarily incompatible, and one can be pursued only at the expense of another, then God's perfect goodness and perfect love are not automatically impugned by pursuing higher goods at the expense of lower goods.

◊ Is it possible that we could be in the position of the ship's dogs? Deeply loved and cared for with a love that surpasses understanding, and yet owing to necessary conditions that generate a conflict between realizing two good states of affairs, our flourishing is thwarted by God for the sake of a higher good and not for our own eventual benefit? If such a thing is not possible, what mistake can be exposed in Tesque's argument to the contrary?

Tesque offers an elementary observation in moral theory. From the fact that someone else is not doing anything morally wrong in performing an action that happens to cause harms to you in particular and perhaps is also even maximizing value from among his alternatives, it does not follow that you are obligated to cooperate with that treatment and participate in bringing about those particular harms. Although he is in no more of a position to insist that such a thing is in fact happening to him than that it is not, Tesque seems to dwell on this thought as one of his reasons for believing his rebellion and abandonment of the Garden could turn out to be justified in the end.

◊ Suppose Tesque is right that he is not morally obligated to cooperate with God if it should turn out that God is sacrificing Tesque's well-being in order to use him as an instrument in the accomplishment of some other divine goal through which he will not ultimately benefit. What other reasons (if any) that Tesque may be neglecting could nevertheless provide compelling grounds for continued obedience and cooperation with God's plan?

Further readings on whether God can morally permissibly make use of us as instruments in order to accomplish divine goals or can permit harms to us that are not ultimately bound up with our own benefit can be found here:

Adams, Marilyn McCord. *Horrendous Evils and the Goodness of God.* Ithaca, NY: Cornell University Press, 1999.

Stump, Eleonore. *Wandering in Darkness: Narrative and the Problem of Suffering.* Oxford: Oxford University Press, 2010.

CHAPTER 4

Divine Deception

At this stage in the story, Tesque has made clear the misery he feels in being separated from all other sentient beings while confined to the Garden. He now reveals the primary consideration he has been contemplating that may provide him with the courage to leave his post and make his way into the world on his own authority and power. This consideration takes the form of one sustained and careful argument for the conclusion that he and you and I have absolutely no idea whether we are being deceived by God on matters of the upmost significance—for example, with respect to the incarnation, the atonement, and the general resurrection.

If Tesque has no good reason to trust what God has supposedly revealed by revelation, no faith in the authority of divine testimony, and no way of determining whether he is nothing but a ship's dog and merely being used for ends that are not his own, perhaps he also has no good reason to continue in obedience to God and would be just as rational to venture out and into the world on his own. At least, he tells both himself and his future daughter (to whom he continues to write his explanatory letter) as much.

There are, of course, two main worries to explore at this juncture.

First—is Tesque correct that lying is not always morally wrong and that for all we know God may have morally justifying reasons to deceive us, and second—if he is correct, do those facts serve as a partial justification for disobedience of the sort he envisions? Let us, in this section, focus on a series of questions in response to the former worry.

Tesque's parable of the boy and the emperor's counselor is designed to show that we can be morally permissibly deceived by an individual who is knowledgeable, wise, and good, and moreover, who deceives as a consequence of his knowledge and goodness.

◊ Is the parable of the boy and the emperor's counselor similar in all relevant respects to the type of divine deception that Tesque is attempting to show may be morally permissible or is there a difference that makes a difference to his attempt to transfer results from one case to the other? If there is, how can it best be exposed?

Tesque considers, in turn, a number of potential responses to the threat of the hypothesis of divine deception, and in accordance with Christian tradition, Tesque takes seriously the claim that we do not come to know truths about matters concerning the incarnation, the atonement, and the general resurrection on the strength of our own natural faculties alone. Rather, our justifying evidence for these tremendously important claims boils down to the foundation of what has been revealed to us by God.

◊ Is this a misreporting of the Christian tradition or is the tradition mistaken on these issues? Can the committed Christian claim that we may come to know independently of divine revelation of the incarnation, the atonement, and the general resurrection?

Tesque further argues that even if we correctly determine that there is disvalue in lying and in being lied to (i.e., that lying brings a characteristic type of evil into the world), God's permitting such an evil is no more or less problematic than the other sorts of evil at issue in the parable of the boy and emperor's counselor.

◊ Can one consistently accept the strategy for defeating the version of the problem of evil that exercises Tesque in chapter 2 and then (without abandoning the elements of that strategy) argue that we can know that this particular type of evil could not be divinely permitted?

Tesque attempts to close off further routes to escape from the argument's unsettling conclusion, including arguing for the truth that deception is sometimes not merely morally permissible but morally obligatory, that traditional bans on lying are often riddled with problematic qualifications, that there seems to be scriptural support for the occasional divine deception, and that deception, while bad, can hardly be elevated to the degree of disvalue found in many other types of evil routinely permitted in world history. Can he be successfully opposed?

◊ Are we in a position to show that lying is always and everywhere an unqualified moral wrong? Are there reasons to think that whereas we can tell the occasional morally permissible lie, depending on our circumstances, relevantly similar circumstances simply could not arise in God's case, perhaps owing to God's omnipotence and omniscience?

Finally, Tesque theorizes on the general conditions under which we can receive knowledge by testimony (or, in this case, by revelation) and argues that there is a special obstacle in the case of divine testimony that cannot be overcome (although, surprisingly, he thinks it can be overcome if the testifier is not divine): Namely, he argues that we cannot satisfy the necessary condition of securing some (non-testimonial) good reason for thinking that God's episodes of testimony are reliable or trustworthy. Tesque's argument thus turns on a particular philosophical thesis about the necessary conditions for receiving knowledge by way of testimony.

◊ Has Tesque imposed too strict a requirement by insisting on this (alleged) necessary condition that he argues we are wholly incapable of satisfying with respect to divine testimony? If not, should we agree that Tesque has successfully proved his point? If so, then what are the correct conditions under which one can acquire knowledge from testimony? Alternatively, is Tesque too quick to regard divine revelation (which, after all, comes in many different forms) as a species of testimony at all?

There is one remaining question the ramifications of which seem to be rather severe. Tesque hesitatingly begins to bring into the open the full scope of the threat that is the current subject of his philosophizing. Suppose he were correct about the possibility of divine deception and about our utter ignorance of whether it occurs and with what frequency and objects.

◊ Would this kind of skepticism quickly spread from grand topics like the general resurrection to everyday, mundane topics, and, indeed, to every topic whatsoever? Can such skepticism be confined once it is unleashed or will it threaten everything, including our ability to identify elementary valid forms of reasoning? If not, why not? If so, how could we retain any confidence in an argument which allegedly demonstrates (among other things) that we have no idea whether we can identify elementary valid forms of reasoning?

Further readings on the hypothesis of divine deception and on the epistemology of testimony can be found here:

Hudson, Hud. "The Father of Lies?" In *Oxford Studies in Philosophy of Religion*, edited by Jonathan Kvanvig, 147–66. Oxford: Oxford University Press, 2014.

Lackey, Jennifer. *Learning from Words: Testimony as a Source of Knowledge.* Oxford: Oxford University Press, 2008.

Wielenberg, Erik. "Sceptical Theism and Divine Lies." *Religious Studies* 46 (2010): 509–23.

CHAPTER 5

Visions from the Tree

Tesque considers the company he is about to keep by reflecting on the angels who fell before him, but is keen to distance himself from them. Somehow his highly abstract and philosophical musings on divine goodness, divine love, and divine deception have morphed into what he now characterizes as his "honorable reasons" for rebellion that surpass in nobleness whatever temptations seduced the previously fallen, and he defensively insists that his own reasons are not "born of pride or lust or vanity or sin."

In the course of this self-promotion, he raises a very puzzling question that has long been debated by those in the Christian tradition who are attracted to the idea of a historical fall. Given the original position of unfallenness, how is the fall so much as possible? It would seem that the conditions under which the (angelic or human) fall could have taken place would require that the creature who falls is already defective in some way or other in order to entertain certain thoughts and temptations, that he is already in the clutches of sin. We will revisit this worry when it again becomes salient in the discussion questions for chapter 10 below.

Tesque pauses from applauding his own fine motives for rebellion, however, to initiate a very important discussion—the discussion of creaturely flourishing or well-being.

Theories of well-being can be hedonistically centered on the quantity and quality of pleasure one experiences, or they can be bound up with how satisfied one is with one's life and its elements and experiences, or they can involve an objective list of goods (which may include some goods in which one has no special interest or pro-attitude), or—as in the case of Tesque's discussion—they can involve an objective list of goods unified by the thought that they contribute to the perfection of a particular kind of creature's nature.

◊ One of the main appeals of subjective theories of well-being is that many people think it is intolerable to maintain that something could be a good for you (in the sense of contributing to your flourishing) unless you have some kind of positive attitude towards it. Does that consideration lead you to favor something like a life-satisfaction view over Tesque's perfectionistic view, or (like Tesque) do you believe that there can be things that contribute to your well-being whether or not you have a pro-attitude towards them?

Tesque offers a partial list of such goods for consideration in which he is guided by thinking about the facts that he is embodied, sentient, possesses intellect and will, and is (or should be) a social creature. Here are his twenty candidates:

Strength, Fitness, Health, Beauty, Achievement, Skill, Power, Exercise of Freedom and Autonomy, Creativity, Contemplation, Joy, Experiences of Pleasure, Aesthetic Appreciation, Knowledge, Virtue, Admiration, Respect, Friendship, Caregiving, Mutual Love

◊ How plausible does this list seem to you as a list of goods for a person that are constitutive of that person's flourishing? Are there entries that you would omit? If so, which and why? Are there items you would have included that Tesque does not mention? If so, what and why?

◊ *An interesting exercise*: rank the twenty items in the order that represents the degree to which they have been goods for you at this current stage of your own life.

It is largely owing to Tesque's felt lack of these goods, especially the social goods, that he takes himself to be exceedingly unhappy and failing to flourish, and it is for the purpose of securing the social goods in particular that he believes have been denied to him that he tells himself it may be worthwhile to rebel against God and vacate the Garden. Although he seems to be dimly aware of the dangers of self-deception where desire is strong, he steels himself against the view that the world he wishes to join is totally corrupt by telling a handful of stories in which he thinks the fallen attempt to struggle admirably against the sins that dominate their lives. His stories illustrate six of the seven deadly sins in turn: wrath, lust, envy, sloth, gluttony, and greed, and in each case he nevertheless purports to find something fine, noble, admirable, good, wondrous, or splendid.

◊ Reread Tesque's six character sketches. Is he right to find in those portrayals something beautiful and worthy of the accolades he bestows on them? How might he find courage in reflecting upon them, as he says he does? Or is Tesque being naïve as he mistakenly draws make-believe lessons from various episodes in the history of humanity and confuses vices with virtues that simply aren't present?

Further readings on theories of happiness and well-being and an introduction to the seven deadly sins can be found here:

Bloomfield, Morton W. *The Seven Deadly Sins.* East Lansing: Michigan State University Press, 1952.

DeYoung, Rebecca Konyndyk. *Glittering Vices*. Grand Rapids: Brazos Press, 2009.

Fletcher, Guy. *The Philosophy of Well-Being: An Introduction*. New York: Routledge, 2016.

Haybron, Daniel. *The Pursuit of Unhappiness: The Elusive Psychology of Well-Being*. Oxford: Oxford University Press, 2008.

CHAPTER 6
Obedience or Rebellion?

Tesque begins to exhibit severe misgivings about his plan for rebellion. Yet he openly continues to agonize over whether or not he should continue to persevere in his duty, given his perceived unhappiness and the intellectual doubts and puzzles to which his philosophical wanderings have given life.

Tesque notes that the abrupt changes which befell the angels who rebelled before him constituted a horror—a transformation of beautiful purity and righteousness into permanent corruption and sinfulness. He even acknowledges that his predecessors thereby made the worst mistake that it was possible for them to make—"to trade eternal happiness for self-elected agony and hopelessness without end."

But then, in the very same breath, he reassures himself that his own reasons are special and importantly different from theirs—that his personal reasons do not have to do with the temptations of pride or inflated self-love. And he rehearses his philosophical conclusions from chapters 3 and 4 to remind himself that even if he knows that God is perfectly good and perfectly loving, he cannot also claim to know that he is not a mere instrument and victim of divine deception.

But how is this cast of mind credible?

◊ How can Tesque confidently impute improper motives, concealed thoughts, malicious desires, and secret vices to others who have rebelled but continue to convince himself that his own motives, thoughts, and desires are virtuous and free from blemish? Can one really go so far as to openly recognize one's own capacity for self-deception (as does Tesque) and acknowledge the debilitating effects which will follow sin (as does Tesque) yet still fully participate in that process of self-deception to the extent that one voluntarily continues to teeter on the brink of ruin while clearly knowing enough to back safely away?

Yet before convincing yourself that such a frame of mind is an outlandish caricature of our own much more mature, sober, and honest processes of introspection and self-awareness, recall that there is an insightful and compelling tradition according to which this is precisely the kind of self-aggrandizing and self-deceptive behavior in which most of us engage a good share of the time.

Further readings on the philosophical and theological cases for the claim that we one and all resemble Tesque to some significant degree in these respects can be found here:

Augustine. *City of God.* Translated by Henry Bettenson. New York: Penguin, 1972.
Pascal, Blaise. *Pensées.* Translated by A. J. Krailsheimer. New York: Penguin, 1995.
Ten Elshof, Gregg. *I Told Me So: Self-Deception and the Christian Life.* Grand Rapids: Eerdmans, 2009.
Wood, William. *Blaise Pascal on Duplicity, Sin, and the Fall: The Secret Instinct.* Oxford: Oxford University Press, 2013.

As the portion of the book that features his character draws to a close, Tesque raises a pointed question not simply about the hope of God's forgiveness should whatever decision he finally makes turn out to be a grave mistake but about the mandatory forgiveness he could expect to receive given God's role in his transgression.

That is, Tesque raises a concern connected to the terribly difficult problem of moral luck. One very popular thesis is that we are morally assessable only for those things which are relevantly under our control; if you have done something morally wrong or if you are responsible or blameworthy for some state of affairs, then you had to possess some significant kind of control over whether the action was performed or over whether the state of affairs obtains. Yet it would seem that sometimes we are charged with wrongdoing or blameworthiness when the action in question was caused by factors outside of our control prior to its occurrence (causal luck) or by features of the circumstances in which we are placed over which we have inadequate control (circumstantial luck) or by aspects of our own character over which we have inadequate control (constitutive luck) or when events that occur after the action is performed over which we have inadequate control (resultant luck) negatively affect the consequences of the action. To the extent that these charges are inconsistent with that popular principle of control just noted, there is pressure to reject these accusations of wrongdoing and responsibility.

Tesque points out that his character was not self-selected but rather determined by God, and to the extent that he is unavoidably driven by his character (perhaps mistakenly) to seek his own good by rushing from the safety and grace of obedience and the Garden into the sin and ruin of rebellion and the fallen world, how can he be held properly responsible for the outcome? Tesque makes his point in terms of constitutive luck, but perhaps he could also appeal to circumstantial luck, given that the sources of his misery seem to be very heavily (and contingently) dependent on the fact that he has spent his entire existence alone in the Garden, bereft of the society and fellowship he so craves.

◊ It seems perfectly clear that Tesque's character and his circumstances contribute significantly to his temptation to disobey and leave the Garden. But is it likewise clear that these factors make succumbing to that temptation something that is outside of Tesque's control? Consider your own case: Are there any actions you have performed which you believe have been determined (and for which you lacked the ability to do otherwise) owing to your character traits or to the circumstances in which you found yourself?

Further readings on the topic of moral luck and on the variety of responses to constitutive and circumstantial luck in particular can be found here:

Statman, Daniel, ed. *Moral Luck.* Albany: State University of New York at Albany Press, 1993.

CHAPTER 7
A Beast Sings

With no introduction or commentary:

◊   What is your take on Lazaraistones?
◊   What of significance did you learn about Tesque in this very brief chapter? How (if at all) has your opinion of Tesque changed after catching a glimpse of him through another character's eyes? Why can't (or doesn't) Tesque see Lazaraistones?
◊   Lazaraistones says, "Hard thoughts are important. I'm pretty sure about that. But I'm also pretty sure that Tesque thinks they are more important than they really are. That's why he always chooses them over all the other things that are good, too. He misses out. I have a much better time on our morning walks." What do you think of the difference of opinion between Tesque and Lazaraistones on the question of the relative value of hard (philosophical/theological) thoughts?

CHAPTER 8
A Night Visitor

As the interlude with Lazaraistones made clear, Naphil is not Tesque's daughter, since he has not yet left the Garden and as of yet has fathered no one. Still, we have the Tree's word that Naphil is someone who nevertheless is in a position to benefit from Tesque's letter (although it was not written to her) and that "she is having difficulties that are similar to Tesque's but different."

Naphil's difficulties are not hard to spot at all. She wears them on her sleeve. As we come to realize that Lazaraistones has brought Tesque's letter to her (perhaps himself confused about her identity but wishing to be helpful to someone in need), we quickly get a very clear sense of just what those difficulties are: Naphil does not like herself, and she is no fan of "the warped and cruel family of man," whose least attractive features she frequently catalogs with real contempt.

She offers several critiques of her fellow human beings. Here is one aimed at you: "Ask anyone whether they have enough leisure time. The answer will to a near certainty be a resounding and self-important *no*. Ask them whether they are well prepared to make use of the leisure time they have. The answer with less certainty (but nevertheless with enough confidence to qualify as an astounding instance of failing to have insight into oneself) will be a somewhat puzzled and self-congratulatory *yes*. O but we are all so very deeply in error in each response."

◊ Naphil is hardly the first person to launch that attack on human beings, but she's committed to it. Did she correctly anticipate your own answers to the questions? Is her evaluation of those answers in error? If so, why?

Naphil is preoccupied with Tesque's letter and flirts with what she clearly takes to be sheer fantasy—namely, that its author is a disgruntled angel who is writing to her and to her alone. Playing along with the conceit and delighting in the coincidences between the content of the missive and her own past, she uses the letter as motivation for putting her own thoughts about her unhappy life in perspective, and she frames those thoughts as a series of responses to Tesque's predicament and arguments. To the extent that it sparks such honest self-reflection, the Tree seemed to be correct that Naphil stands some chance of being genuinely benefitted by receiving Tesque's letter. But what should we make of the Tree's other remark reported by Lazaraistones in the previous chapter?

◊ Whereas Tesque's leading complaint is lack of access to others and the misery of solitude, Naphil's grievance against the world is the presence of others and the unavailability of solitude. Thus differing in such a stark and dramatic way, how can the Tree be right in suggesting that their difficulties are actually quite similar to one another?

In thinking about this question, it may be helpful to read one or both of the pieces cited below on the deadly sin of sloth. Despite the modern-day connotations of mere laziness and indolence, sloth is a deadening and dangerous depression which can overwhelm and extinguish the normal range of one's emotional response to life. Sloth is the sin which carves out joy, leaving in its place a hollow and vacant indifference (even to items and activities one judges intellectually to be goods), and which gradually robs its victim of the capacity to fight his or her way back to happiness and well-being. Sloth is an indifference to goods which can transform into despair. It is less a disordered desire than an extinguished desire, and it is accompanied by a resistance to the duties appropriate to nurturing loving relationships.

Even if Tesque and Naphil each manifest some version of sloth, here is one significant difference that distinguishes them: unlike Tesque, Naphil can see Lazaraistones (on whom she bestows the name *Joy*) even if she cannot fully recognize him for what he is.

Further readings on the deadly sin of sloth and its characterization as a resistance to the demands of love can be found here:

DeYoung, Rebecca Konyndyk. "Sloth: Some Historical Reflections on Laziness, Effort, and Resistance to the Demands of Love." In *Virtues and Their Vices*. Edited by Kevin Timpe and Craig A. Boyd, 177–98. Oxford: Oxford University Press, 2014.
Fairlie, Henry. *The Seven Deadly Sins Today*. Notre Dame, IN: University of Notre Dame Press, 1979.

CHAPTER 9
Misanthropy

Naphil commences her long series of point-by-point rebuttals to Tesque's letter. In addition to minor sparring over the pleasures and pains of the presence of others, she critically evaluates Tesque's three primary theses from chapters 2, 3, and 4. But first a comment about method:

◊ Naphil points out that Tesque's parable of the Lazarai Stones is something he simply made up (or at least she can find no evidence for the existence of the relevant people and their legends). If it is made up—and far less realistic than, say, the parable of the boy and the emperor's counselor from chapter 4—would that fact have any bearing whatsoever on whether it has the power to achieve its goal in undermining a particular argument for atheism?

Naphil takes issue with Tesque's first reason for maintaining that we should not believe the conditional bridge premise about the Lazarai Stones. Tesque seems to argue that, if we are in the dark about whether it is likely that if there were Lazarai Stones, then they would be in a location in which the villagers could not search—then we should not accept the bridge premise. Naphil argues that this is too weak, suggesting instead this replacement: If we have a good reason to think that it is likely that if there were Lazarai Stones, then they would be in a location in which the villagers could not search—then we should not accept the bridge premise.

◊ Take a moment to appreciate the difference between Tesque's sentence and Naphil's suggested replacement. Is Naphil right that Tesque makes things too easy on himself by merely pointing out that we have no idea what to say about that probability? In order for Tesque's first reason to be successful, do we need to adopt the stronger view that we have good reason to endorse that probability?

Naphil takes a turn at extending Tesque's story about the Lazarai Stones with what we can call the parable of Hubris, the seer, and in so doing represents yet another popular style of atheistic argument that manages to bypass the troublesome bridge-premise which was the main target of Tesque's original complaint.

◊ What is the parable of Hubris, the seer? Is the parable of Hubris, the seer similar in all relevant respects to the new strategy for denying the existence of morally justifying reasons (for permitting evil) that Naphil is attempting to critique or is there a difference that makes a difference to her attempt to transfer results from one case to the other? If there is, how can it best be exposed?

Despite a good deal of common ground, a serious theological disagreement surfaces in Naphil's next remarks. She notes that the two of them agree God is perfectly good and perfectly loving and that they agree on the details of the analyses Tesque put forward of each of those divine attributes. Moreover, they agree that neither feature would require God to break silence or emerge from hiding or reveal himself in any way or even always act in our best interests, despite the ardent and incessant desire of his creatures to find security and comfort in his presence. Their startling difference has to do with the objects of God's love. Tesque believes that God loves humanity and Naphil denies this. The reason is that Naphil believes the fallen have so effaced the image of God in which they were made that they have polluted themselves with sin and have made themselves unlovable. And, of course, she seems to have no shortage of reasons why human beings are an unlovable lot; she has spent a lifetime accumulating evidence on that score.

◊ What are the prospects for Naphil's view that human beings, steeped in sin, have made themselves unworthy objects of love, and that it would be an intolerable defect of love (impossible in a God of perfect love) to love the unlovable? The atonement, as she argues, can still be motivated by God's love, but for what human beings once were and for what they can be again, not for what they have made of themselves in their present state of rebellion. If Tesque is correct and Naphil is mistaken, what, exactly, is the reason explaining God's love for humanity *during* its fallen state?

Naphil is a self-professed misanthrope, and she does not exempt herself from the general disdain and contempt she has for humanity. In thus hating (in a sense) her neighbor, she seems to be about as far from satisfying the second great love commandment as it is possible to be. Yet she denies this in saying "the second and lesser of the love commandments I finesse. I love my neighbor exactly as I love myself and exactly as we both deserve to be loved—not at all."

◊ If this remark is to be taken seriously, it suggests that Naphil hears the command to love her neighbor as herself as little more than the command not to privilege herself and her interests over her neighbor by indulging in inordinate and disproportional self-love. And perhaps also as the command to match her loves to the worthiness of their objects. These goals she claims to achieve. Is that a sufficient reading of the command? If not, what is the best way to express exactly what is missing in that interpretation?

Unapologetic for her misanthropy, Naphil mounts a case for the appropriateness of a general attitude of disdain and contempt for the collective behavior and character of her fellow humans.

◊ If there is something virtuous about forming and nurturing the right pro-attitudes towards states of affairs with value and the right negative attitudes toward states of affairs with disvalue, then is there any truth to Naphil's claim that misanthropy has been mislabeled as a vice? Is she mistaken in the faults and failures and cruelties she purports to find in abundance in humanity? If so, in what ways? If not, why should she replace her present attitudes which hold in contempt contemptible features with attitudes of love?

Divine deception is the one aspect of Tesque's letter that most captivates Naphil's attention, and her initial reaction takes the form of a well-known style of rebuttal that is often thought to somehow involve an unfair dialectical move. She confesses she cannot spot the mistake in reasoning, but simply declares—"I'll bet you're wrong." Perhaps this comes from her independent reasons for thinking the conclusion of the argument must be false, reasons that stress the uncontainable scope of such skepticism and the instability of the conclusion. (That is, Naphil explores in some depth the repercussions hinted at in the second question on p. 132.)

There is a style of refutation known as the G. E. Moore Shift. When an argument is valid, its premises entail its conclusion. But that also guarantees that if its conclusion is false, then at least one of its premises is also false. When confronted, then, with a valid argument, one always faces a choice: Is the denial of the conclusion more plausible than the conjunction of the premises? If one thinks the answer is *yes*, the argument can be turned on its head, as it were, and declared a failure even without spotting the particular mistake that the argument commits.

◊ Is it plausible to see Naphil's response to Tesque's argument for the possibility of divine deception as an instance of the G. E. Moore Shift? Do you think this is an acceptable form of refutation even if, as she admits, she cannot spot the flaw in Tesque's reasoning? Whether the form is acceptable or not, do you think her comments about the instability of the conclusion really do show that the denial of the conclusion is more plausible than the case that Tesque has made for the premises of the argument?

Further readings on the nature of divine love, on misanthropy, and on the G. E. Moore Shift can be found here:

Gibson, Andrew. *Misanthropy: The Critique of Humanity*. London: Bloomsbury Academic, 2017.

Stump, Eleonore. *Wandering in Darkness: Narrative and the Problem of Suffering*. Oxford: Oxford University Press, 2010.

The 21st Century Monads. "The G. E. Moore Shift." https://the21stcenturymonads.net/#videos, 2009. Retrieved from: https://www.listennotes.com/podcasts/the-21st-century/the-g-e-moore-shift-ugqkVe4d62W/.

CHAPTER 10

O Infelix Culpa

Philosophical skirmishes on evil, hiddenness, and deception now set to one side, Naphil's letter of response to Tesque takes a dark turn. Naphil will have none of Tesque's charitable attempts to find virtue and nobility in humanity's struggle with sin, as becomes clear in her invitation to co-author his six character sketches from chapter 5. Exactly where Tesque purports to find something fine, noble, admirable, good, wondrous, or splendid, Naphil finds disordered cravings for interpersonal power, for sexual domination, for social authority, for prestige and applause, for control over the environment, and for unlimited information.

◊ Where Tesque seems to see broken individuals bravely attempting to rise above their circumstances to pursue justice and virtue and meaningful interpersonal relationships, Naphil seems to see selfish and self-absorbed individuals locked in competition for scarce resources, each trying to advance his or her own cause at the expense of the others. Who do you tend to side with in these exchanges on the primary motivations in human nature and why? Does it matter that Tesque comes to his opinions while actively seeking justification for his own contemplated act of disobedience and sin?

Naphil then completes Tesque's tour of the sins with her accusation that Tesque himself suffers from a kind of pride or at least from its precursor (but more on that distinction in a moment). She underscores and amplifies his own misgivings about the dangers of carrying out his plan and ridicules as absurd his apparent confidence that his motives are untainted and that he will be capable of succeeding on his own power once separated from God (as he most certainly will be should he choose the path of disobedience). Her brief lecture on the dangers of self-deception has one peculiar feature, however. Whereas she has little problem uncovering Tesque's susceptibility to self-deception, she does not seem to consider the prospect that she may suffer from the same malady.

Tesque repeatedly insists that his unhappiness will be lifted and his well-being secured if he can only enter into the fellowship with others that he has been denied for so long. In fact, he is so desperate to experience love of neighbor that he has talked himself into the thought that disobedience to God may be the best route to that end. Naphil reverses this prediction and insists that her unhappiness will be lifted and her well-being secured if she can only escape the society of her fellow creatures and focus exclusively and privately on her single-minded love of God.

◊ Each of our characters continually experiences a deep and penetrating sadness. Each has become indifferent to genuine goods in the world and is deeply resistant to the demands of love. Each seems convinced that the other already possesses exactly what one needs to achieve well-being and happiness. And each is willing to trade away precisely what the other covets in order to occupy the one-sided condition the other finds miserable. Perhaps Tesque is guilty of self-deception in this process. Can that charge also be justly leveled against Naphil?

Naphil voices a suspicion about Tesque closely related to an earlier question Tesque raised about his predecessors, the fallen angels, in chapter 5. Tesque's puzzle was how it is possible for anyone to fall at all, given one's initial condition of innocence and grace. It would seem that one would already have to be in bondage to sin in order to succumb to the temptations of rebellion. How, for example, can one engage in a first act of disobedience *from* the vice of pride, if the presence of pride already is an expression of sin? Must there be a pre-fall, prior to a fall, and so an infinite regress? Naphil's puzzle is connected to this theme. How can Tesque genuinely be an unfallen creature on the verge of his primal act of disobedience when his letter seems to reveal (as Naphil puts it) "a mixture of arrogance, self-absorption, vanity, and self-deception," the very trappings of the noetic effects of sin where (by hypothesis) there has of yet been no sin?

Naphil offers a tentative solution to these puzzles which is Kierkegaardian in spirit. As Milton's God declares in Book III of *Paradise Lost*, creatures were made "just and right; sufficient to have stood, though free to fall." Tesque has been given the gift of free will—the freedom to obey and the freedom to disobey, and Naphil argues that the puzzling prerequisite of a fall can best be explained by appeal to the psychological features that necessarily attend the consciousness of morally significant freedom. Such freedom breeds a kind of *anxiety*, an unsettledness in the recognition that some facts about the world are solely up to you, a terrifying realization that the decision to obey or not to obey (with all its consequences) is yours and yours alone. Given the gift of freedom, you will shape the world in at least one unalterable and magnificent or tragic way, and no one can wrest that control from you or force your hand. In this one respect, you are a co-creator with God.

◊ Do you find it plausible that this appeal to the anxiety that accompanies the consciousness of freedom might serve as an adequate explanation of the possibility of a fall into sin? Such anxiety when operative in a pre-fallen state need not be classified among the noetic effects of sin (for, by hypothesis, there is as of yet no sin to cause such effects), but it can nevertheless mimic some of the later noetic effects of sin, raising certain states of affairs to the status of temptations and sufficiently clouding the intellect and the will to make disobedience a salient possibility.

As the portion of the book that features her character draws to a close, Naphil tells a final story which she describes as a blueprint, within whose roughly drawn lines all the stories ever to be fashioned in our world must somewhere reside. Reread Naphil's story that begins with the words "Creation groans with the consequences of disobedience" and ends with the words "Horrors alone await you here." Naphil's story is an expression of what can be called the philosophy of pessimism—a general thesis according to which creation, its kingdom of animals, its rational inhabitants, and its social institutions are absolutely shot through with disvalue and suffering, and according to which there is very little reason to be optimistic about genuine progress or improvement as the future unfolds.

◊ The Enlightenment was famous for a counter-thesis of optimism, but history is full of poets and philosophers, tragedians and theologians, aphorists and political theorists who side with Naphil. Where do you locate yourself in this debate and why?

Further readings on the concept of anxiety and on the philosophy of pessimism can be found here:

Dienstag, Joshua Foa. *Pessimism: Philosophy, Ethic, Spirit.* Princeton, NJ: Princeton University Press, 2006.

Hudson, Hud. *Fallenness and Well-Being.* Oxford: Oxford University Press, forthcoming.

Tanner, John S. *Anxiety in Eden: A Kierkegaardian Reading of Paradise Lost.* Oxford: Oxford University Press, 1992.

CHAPTER II
Return to the Garden

In the opening sentence of the introduction to this work, I suggested that *A Grotesque in the Garden* is a story of two spiritual mistakes. I believe the final three paragraphs of chapter 11 confirm this judgment. The reader, of course, can decide for him or herself.

One reading of the final sentence of the novel is a summary of its main theme—there can be no true or lasting joy without both love of God and love of neighbor. But Joy (as opposed to joy) is a character with all the requisite capacities of personhood—a cognitive and affective being possessed of an intellect and a will and engaged in his own unique and precious relationship with God quite apart from whatever function he may also have been playing with respect to God's other purposes involving Tesque and Naphil.

◊ Why, then, is Joy released by the divine hand and no longer attended to by the divine mind? How can God let him perish?

If this question were put to Tesque, how would he answer? If this question were put to Naphil, how would she answer? When the question is put to you, how do you answer?

Acknowledgments

I am indebted to several persons and to some institutions. I extend my thanks to Western Washington University and to its department of philosophy for treating me so very well over the last quarter century and for providing me with the time and resources to work on projects like this one. I also extend my thanks to the philosophy departments at Baylor University, Boise State University, Peking University, Purdue University, the University of Leeds, the University of Notre Dame, the University of Southern California, the University of Virginia, and Westmont College, as well as to the Center for Philosophy of Religion at the University of Notre Dame, Fuller Theological Seminary, and the John Templeton Foundation for financial support and for opportunities to give colloquium and conference presentations directly related to a number of the philosophical topics at issue in the story. Finally, I would like to acknowledge that Tesque's speech on divine deception has an ancestor in one of my previous academic essays, "The Father of Lies?" *Oxford Studies in Philosophy of Religion*, ed. Jonathan Kvanvig (Oxford University Press, 2014), 147–66.

I am also delighted to have the opportunity to thank colleagues and friends who over the years have generously offered insightful conversation on issues directly related to this project: William J. Abraham, Elizabeth Barnes, Bear the Shih Tzu, Matt Benton, Mike Bergmann, Jeff Brower, Godehard Brüntrup, Lara Buchak, Ross Cameron, Robin Collins, Andrew Cortens, Oliver Crisp, Richard Cross, Helen De Cruz, Kevin Diller, Trent Dougherty, Paul Draper, Paul Dunn, Evan Fales, Peter Forrest, Tyron Goldschmidt, Cathi

Hepker, Daniel Howard-Snyder, Frances Howard-Snyder, Joseph Jedwab, Shieva Kleinschmidt, Andrew Knapp, Jonathan Kvanvig, Sam Lebens, Christian Lee, Brian Leftow, Robin Le Poidevin, Hans Madueme, Neil Manson, Ned Markosian, Kris McDaniel, Trenton Merricks, Bradley Monton, Sam Newlands, Timothy O'Connor, Timothy Pawl, Dee Payton, Guo Peng, John Pittard, Alvin Plantinga, Alex Pruss, Josh Rasmussen, Mike Rea, Bradley Rettler, Blake Roeber, Jeffrey Russell, John Schellenberg, Tom Senor, Amy Seymour, Ge Siyou, Joshua Spencer, Eleonore Stump, Meghan Sullivan, James Taylor, Neal Tognazzini, Jason Turner, David Vander Laan, Christina van Dyke, Peter van Inwagen, Jerry Walls, Ryan Wasserman, Dennis Whitcomb, Robbie Williams, Roger White, Ed Wierenga, Sameer Yadav, and Dean Zimmerman.